我渴望发出健康之光、愉悦之光、沉静的勇气之光、美好的愿望之光。我祈望简单、诚实、率真、自然天成、身心洁净、不加矫饰——泰然自若、无所畏惧地去面对任何阻碍，去迎接每一个困难。

I desire to radiate health, cheerfulness, calm courage and good will. I wish to be simple, honest, frank, natural, clean in mind and clean in body, unaffected—to face any obstacle and meet every difficulty unabashed and unafraid.

一个人，也能有好时光

冯铃之／编译

江苏人民出版社

图书在版编目（CIP）数据

一个人，也能有好时光：英汉对照 / 冯铃之编译. --
南京：江苏人民出版社，2016.1
ISBN 978-7-214-17088-0

Ⅰ. ①一… Ⅱ. ①冯… Ⅲ. ①英语—汉语—对照读物 Ⅳ. ①H319.4

中国版本图书馆CIP数据核字（2015）第311262号

书　　名	一个人，也能有好时光：英汉对照
编 译 者	冯铃之
责任编辑	朱　超
装帧设计	浪殿设计　飞　扬
版式设计	张文艺
出版发行	凤凰出版传媒股份有限公司 江苏人民出版社
出版社地址	南京市湖南路1号A楼，邮编：210009
出版社网址	http://www.jspph.com http://jsrmcbs.tmall.com
经　　销	凤凰出版传媒股份有限公司
印　　刷	北京中印联印务有限公司
开　　本	718毫米×1000毫米 1/16
印　　张	12
字　　数	159千字
版　　次	2016年5月第1版　2016年5月第1次印刷
标准书号	978-7-214-17088-0
定　　价	24.00元

Enjoy the Loneliness Alone

一个人，也能有好时光

A Morning Wish
清晨许愿

◎ W.R. Hunt

The sun is just rising in the morning of another day. What can I wish that this day may bring me? Nothing that shall make the world or others poorer, nothing at the expense of other men; but just those few things which in their coming do not stop me but touch me rather, as they pass and gather strength.

I wish that this day could bring me a few friends, who understand me, and yet remain my friends; I also wish that this day could bring me a work to do which has real value.

I wish that this day could bring me a mind unafraid to travel, even though the trail be not blazed, and I wish that this day could bring me an understanding heart.

I wish that this day could bring me a sight of the eternal hills, and the blue sea stretching to the horizon, and of something beautiful which the hands of men have made.

I wish that this day could bring me a sense of humor, and the power to laugh, a little leisure with nothing to do.

And I crave for a few moments of quiet, silent meditation in the morning of this day.

朝阳照常在又一个清晨缓缓升起。我该期望这一天带给我什么呢？我希望它所带给我的不会让世界或他人更贫穷，不会牺牲他人；而是那些微小的、能触动我的东西，在它们经过时、聚集力量时，不会妨碍我。

我期望这一天能够带给我几个理解我的朋友，并且我们的友谊天长地久；我期望这一天能够带给我一份真正有价值的工作。

我期望这一天能够带给我一颗无畏的远行的心，即使旅途没有光亮的照耀；我期望这一天能够带给我一颗善解人意的心。

我期望这一天能够让我看到永恒的山脉，一望无际的海洋，看到人类亲手创造的美好事物。

我期望这一天能够带给我幽默感，带给我大笑的力量，以及一点点无所事事的闲暇时光。

在这一天的清晨，我渴望得到片刻的宁静和沉思。

目 录 | CONTENTS

彼岸难得，知足常乐

记忆永恒，寂寞也美

点滴改变，收获精彩

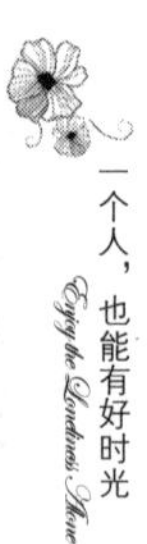

爱在转角，拥抱幸福

彼岸难得，知足常乐

Almost any situation—good or bad—is affected by the attitude we bring to.

差不多任何一种处境——无论是好是坏——都受到我们对待处境的态度的影响。

The Trees Outside My Window
窗外的风景

◎ Bonnie

From the window of my room, I could see a tall cotton-rose hibiscus. In spring, when green foliage was half hidden by mist, the tree looked very enchanting dotted with red blossom. This inspiring neighbor of mine often set my mind working. I gradually regarded it as my best friend.

Nevertheless, when I opened the window one morning, to my amazement, the tree was almost bare beyond recognition as a result of the storm ravages the night before. Struck by the plight, I was seized with a sadness at the thought "all the blossom is doomed to fall". I could not help sighing with emotion: the course of life never runs smooth, for there are so many ups and downs, twists and turns. The vicissitudes of my life saw my beloved friends parting one after another. Isn't it similar to the tree shedding its flowers in the wind?

This event faded from my memory as time went by. One day after I came home from the countryside, I found the room stuffy and casually opened the window. Something outside caught my eye and dazzled me. It was a plum tree all scarlet with blossom set off beautifully by the sunset. The surprise discovery overwhelmed me with pleasure. I wondered why I had no idea of some unyielding life sprouting over the fallen petals when I was grieving for the

名人语库

As fruit needs not only sunshine but cold nights and chilling showers to ripen it, so character needs not only joy but trial and difficulty to mellow it.

Hugh Black

正如水果不仅需要阳光，也需要凉夜一样，寒冷的雨水能使其成熟。人的性格陶冶不仅需要欢乐，也需要考验和困难。

休·布莱克（美国作家）

从我房间的窗户往外看，可以看到一株高大的芙蓉。春天时，绿树在薄雾中若隐若现，点缀着朵朵红花，样子十分迷人。这位邻居总是开启我的灵感，让我思如泉涌。渐渐地，我就把它当成我最好的朋友了。

然而，一天早晨，当我推开窗户时，却惊诧地发现，这株芙蓉已经被前夜的风暴摧残得面目全非，变得叶落枝残。震惊之余，一种“繁花落尽”的悲凉之感在我的心头油然而生。我不禁感慨道：人生从来都不是一帆风顺的，生命中总会有那么多的跌宕起伏、坎坷挫折。我挚爱的朋友一个个离我而去，一切都见证着生命的变化无常。这不正像这随风逝去的花吗?

随着时间的推移，这件事渐渐淡出了我的记忆。一天，当我从郊外回到家后，感觉房间很闷，便推开了窗。就在这一瞬间，窗外一片繁荣的景象让我惊呆了。梅树开满了一簇簇火红的花朵，与落日暮霭相映成趣，格外美丽。这意外的发现让我欣喜不已。我从没想过，当我正因花落叶残而

hibiscus.

When the last withered petal dropped, all the joyful admiration for the hibiscus sank into oblivion as if nothing was left, until the landscape was again ablaze with the red plum blossom to remind people of life's alternation and continuance. Can't it be said that life is actually a symphony, a harmonious composition of loss and gain.

Standing by the window lost in thought for a long time, I realized that no scenery in the world remains unchanged. As long as you keep your heart basking in the sun, every dawn will present a fine prospect for you to unfold and the world will always be about new hopes.

悲伤之时，它竟然还藏着如此顽强的生命。

当芙蓉的最后一片花瓣枯萎凋零时，人们对它的欣喜和赞美也随之飘散，消逝得无影无踪。而现在，梅树却成长起来，那火红的花儿向人们昭示着生命的更迭与延续。谁能否认生命就是一部得失共存的和谐交响曲呢?

我站在窗前沉思良久，突然意识到，世界上没有一成不变的风景。只要你的心中充满阳光，那么每个黎明都会为你展现出一片由你开启的美好前景，整个世界都将充满新的希望。

Gratitude to Be Grateful
彼岸无尽头，知足才长乐

◎ Allen Iverson

Many people believe that they will be happy once they arrive at some specific goal they set for themselves. However, more often than not, once you arrive "there" you will still feel dissatisfied, and move your "there" vision to yet another point in the future. By always chasing after another "there", you are never really appreciating what you already have right "here". It is important for human beings to keep sober-minded about the age-old drive to look beyond the place where you now stand. On one hand, your life is enhanced by your dreams and aspirations. On the other hand, these drives can pull you farther and farther from your enjoyment of your life right now. By learning the lessons of gratitude and abundance, you can bring yourself closer to fulfilling the challenge of living in the present.

Gratitude

To be grateful means you are thankful for and appreciative of what you have and where you are on your path right now. Gratitude fills your heart with the joyful feeling and allows you to fully appreciate everything that arises on your path. As you strive to keep your focus on the present moment, you can

名人语库

Have no fear of perfection—you'll never reach it.

Salvador Dali

不要为十全十美担心——你永远做不到十全十美。

萨尔瓦多·达利（西班牙画家）

许多人都相信，一旦他们达到了自己所设定的某个特定目标，他们就会快乐。然而，更多的事实往往是，当你到达“彼岸”时，你仍然会感到不满足，并且将你的“彼岸”指向未来的另一个景象。始终追求一个又一个的“彼岸”，你永远都无法欣赏到你已经到达的“此处”。对于人们来说，不安现状的欲望存在已久，但更重要的是应保持头脑清醒。一方面，你的生活因为梦想和渴望而更加精彩。另一方面，这些欲望又使你越来越不懂得珍惜和享受现在所拥有的生活。通过学习感恩和知足这一课，你会离战胜当下生活中的挑战更进一步。

感恩

感恩是指你感谢、珍惜你所拥有的一切，以及你目前所处的人生境遇。心中充满感激之情，你的心灵就会充满愉悦，你就能充分领悟到人生道路上的一切经历。如果你把眼光聚焦在此时此刻，你就能感受到在“此处”

experience the full wonder of "here".

There are many ways to cultivate gratitude. Here are just a few suggestions you may wish to try:

1. Imagine what your life would be like if you lost all that you had. This will most surely remind you of how much you do appreciate it.

2. Make a list each day of all that you are grateful for, so that you can stay conscious daily of your blessings. Do this especially when you are feeling as though you have nothing to feel grateful for. Or spend a few minutes before you go to sleep giving thanks for all that you have.

3. Spend time offering assistance to those who are less fortunate than you, so that you may gain perspective.

However you choose to learn gratitude is irrelevant. What really matters is that you create a space in your consciousness for appreciation for all that you have right now, so that you may live more joyously in your present moment.

Abundance

One of the most common human fears is scarcity. Many people are afraid of not having enough of what they need or want, and so they are always striving to get to a point when they would finally have enough.

Alan and Linda always dreamed of living "the good life". Both from poor working-class families, they married young and set out to fulfill their mutual goal of becoming wealthy. They both worked very hard for years, amassing a small fortune, so they could move from their two-bedroom home to a palatial seven-bedroom home in the most upscale neighborhood. They focused their energies on accumulating all the things they believed signified abundance: membership in the local exclusive country club, luxury cars, designer clothing, and high-

的美妙之处。

有许多方法可以培养感恩之心，以下这些建议不妨试试看：

1. 想象如果你失去了你所拥有的一切，你的生活将会怎么样。这一定会让你想起，原来你有多么感激现在的一切。

2. 每天列出所有值得你心存感激的事，这样每天你都能意识到自己的幸运。坚持这样做，尤其是当你感觉似乎没什么可感激的时候。或者，在睡觉前花几分钟时间，感谢你所拥有的一切。

3. 花些时间，去帮助那些没你这么幸运的人，这样你或许会对生活有新的认识。

事实上，你选择怎样的方法去学习感恩，这无关紧要。真正重要的是，你应该有意识地去感激你所拥有的一切，这样你就能更快乐地享受当下。

知足常乐

人类最普遍的恐惧之一就是贫穷。许多人担心他们的所需所求不够，所以他们总是努力使自己最终能拥有一切。

艾伦和琳达总是梦想着能过上“好日子”。他们都来自于贫困的工薪阶层家庭，年纪轻轻就早早结了婚，然后开始为他们共同的致富目标而努力。他们拼命工作了很多年，积累了一些资金，然后就从两居室搬到了一所高档社区的富丽堂皇的七居室大房子。此后，他们把精力都放在那些他们以为是代表富足的事情上：当地惟一的一家乡村俱乐部的会员资格，豪华轿车，名牌服装，上流社会的朋友。但是，无论他们积累了多少财富，似乎

class society friends. No matter how much they accumulated, however, it never seemed to be enough. They were unable to erase the deep fear of scarcity both had acquired in childhood.

Indeed, they needed to learn the lesson of abundance. Then the stock market crashed in 1987, and Alan and Linda lost a considerable amount of money. A bizarre but costly lawsuit depleted another huge portion of their savings. One thing led to another, and they found themselves in a financial disaster. Assets needed to be sold, and eventually they lost the country club membership, the cars, and the house. It took several years and much hard work for Alan and Linda to land on their feet, and though they now live a life far from extravagant, they have taken stock of their lives and feel quite blessed. Only now, as they assess what they have left—a solid, loving marriage, their health, a dependable income, and good friends—do they realize that true abundance comes not from amassing, but rather from appreciating.

Scarcity consciousness arises as a result of the "hole-in-the-soul syndrome". This is when we attempt to fill the gaps in our inner lives with things from the outside world. But like puzzle pieces, you can't fit something in where it does not naturally belong. No amount of external objects, affection, love, or attention can ever fill an inner void. We already have enough, so we should revel in our own interior abundance.

都是不足够的。他们无法抹去童年时代因贫穷而产生的深刻恐惧感。

事实上，他们就需要学会知足常乐这一课。1987 年股市暴跌，艾伦和琳达损失了一大笔钱。一场莫名其妙的昂贵的官司又耗尽了他们另一大笔积蓄。这一件接一件的祸事，导致他们陷入了经济危机之中。他们不得不变卖资产，最终失去了乡村俱乐部的会员资格、汽车和房子。他们花了好几年的时间，才努力从困境中走出来，尽管他们现在已经远离奢侈，但他们主宰着自己的生活，感到幸运又知足。只有此刻，他们才掂量着尚未远离的一切——坚固相爱的婚姻、健康的身体、稳定的收入、真正的朋友等——他们终于意识到，真正的富足并非来自于财富的积累，而是来自于感激和珍惜。

贫穷感产生于“精神空虚综合症”，也就是我们试图用外界之物来填补内心的空虚。但是，就像拼图游戏一样，你不能把它硬放在原本不属于它的位置上。任何身外之物、感情、爱或关注，都无法填补内心的空虚。我们拥有的已经足够，因此，我们应满足于内心世界的丰富与充实。

Listen to Your Inner Voice
倾听你内心的声音

◎ William Howard

Is there inside you? Very much, ever since you were brought into this world. When you couldn't open your mouth till the first two years on planet earth, inner voice is the one through which you interpreted and understood things.

Inner voice is the voice mouth of the subconscious mind. The subconscious mind is always acting as a secondary reflector of thoughts and ideas in the body. It justifies and rationalizes what is right and what is wrong. When we go against what the inner voice say we get a guilty conscious and are bothered by it throughout our lives.

At times when we are feeling low or those unforgettable moments when we are let down, we seem to need some kind of emotional or mental support. We usually speak to our closest pal or our dearest family member during times of distress to ease the burden. At such times we get over the initial drizzle of emotional anxiety and mental restlessness, because of the pepping up by our empathic listener. We suddenly feel rejuvenated because our inner voice alerts us to get on with things and leave the things of past on the memory books of our brain.

The inner voice is always right most of the times because it knows us better

名人语库

Most folks are about as happy as they make up their minds to be.

Abraham Lincoln

对于大多数人来说，他们认定自己有多幸福，就有多幸福。

亚伯拉罕·林肯（美国总统）

你的内心深处有呼之欲出的声音吗？是的，自从你来到这个世界上，你的心灵就在不断地诉说。来到世上的最初两年时，你还不能开口说话，而心灵的声音就是你理解这个世界的通道。

内心的声音是潜意识诉说的嘴。潜意识一直是思想和观点的二次映射。它证明且控制着事物的对与错。当我们违背了内心的声音，我们会有一种负罪感，而且在余生中总会因它所困扰。

当我们情绪低落或灰心丧气时，我们似乎就需要某种情绪或精神上的支持。通常在痛苦的时候，我们会向最好的朋友或家人诉说，以此减轻压力。在这样的时刻，我们克服了不安和焦虑的情绪，因为有了为我们打气的听众。我们迅速恢复了活力，因为我们内心的声音在提醒我们，继续走下去，将过去的那些烦恼都留在回忆里吧。

大多时候，内心的声音总是对的，因为它比任何人都要了解我们，甚

than others and probably even ourselves. It is the dare devil child of the intuitions which we have been having since childhood. It's good to go by intuitions most of the times because it's the response provided due to the synchronism between our mental and physical being.

Whenever you are trying your first cigarette, or whenever you are asked to take sides in an argument, you are always in a sense of dilemma. During these times your inner voice automatically gives its verdict, which when over written, might leave us unhappy in the future. It's up to us to either ignore the morale booster inside us or go out to the world and search for spiritual guru's and happiness, when all these things are very much present within us.

至超过我们自己。它是我们从小就一直伴随我们直觉的冒失小鬼。遵从直觉是有好处的，因为它大多是来自于我们的精神和现实之间同步的反应。

当你尝试去抽第一支烟的时候，或者当你被要求在某个争论里站在某一方的时候，你总是会感觉到困扰。在这些时刻，你内心的声音会自动给出裁决，甚至夸大来说，会给我们的将来留下不快。当这些事摆在眼前的时候，我们该决定是忽略内心的冲动，还是走向世界，去寻找精神领袖和幸福。

The 10 Essential Habits of Positive People
乐观人群的 10 个好习惯

© Judy Belmont

Are you waiting for life events to turn out the way you want so that you can feel more positive about your life? Do you find yourself having pre-conditions to your sense of well-being, thinking that certain things must happen for you to be happier? Do you think there is no way that your life stresses can make you anything other than "stressed out" and that other people just don't understand?

If your answer is "yes" to any of these questions, you might find yourself lingering in the land of negativity for too long!

The following are some tips to keep positive no matter what comes your way. This article will help you stop looking for what psychologists call "positivity" in all the wrong places! Here are the ten essential habits of positive people.

1. Positive people don't confuse quitting with letting go

Instead of hanging on to ideas, beliefs, and even people that are no longer healthy for them, they trust their judgment to let go of negative forces in their lives. Especially in terms of relationships, they subscribe to the phinciples which goes:

I will grant myself the ability to trust the healthy people in my life;

名人语库

Optimist: A man who gets treed by a lion but enjoys the scenery.

W. Winchell

乐观主义者：被狮子逼上了树但仍能欣赏风景的人。

华尔特·温切尔（美国评论家、演员）

你是否在等待发生什么可以改变命运的大事件，借此过上自己想要的生活，这样你才能更积极地对待生活？你是否发现自己的幸福感是有条件的，认为必须发生某些事才能让你更快乐？你是否认为自己的生活压力过大，除了“紧张”以外别无他法，而其他人都无法理解？

如果你对以上任何一个问题回答了“是”，你可能已经在消极情绪中沉溺太久！

以下是一些无论遇到何事都能保持乐观的小窍门。这篇文章将帮助你避免不当地寻找心理学家所说的“积极性”。来看看乐观人群必有的 10 个好习惯。

1. 乐观人群懂得放手与顺其自然的区别

乐观人群不会纠结于那些会给他们带来负面影响的思想、信仰，甚至是人，他们相信自己的判断，会让生活中的负面压力顺其自然。尤其是在人际关系方面，他们认可这样的原则：

对于给我的生活带来积极影响的人，我会尽我所能去信任他们；

To set limits with, or let go of, the negative ones;

And to have the wisdom to know the difference!

2. Positive people don't just have a good day—they make a good day

Waiting, hoping and wishing seldom have a place in the vocabulary of positive individuals. Rather, they use strong words that are pro-active and not reactive. Passivity leads to a lack of involvement, while positive people get very involved in constructing their lives. They work to make changes to feel better in tough times rather than wish their feelings away.

3. For the positive person, the past stays in the past

Good and bad memories alike stay where they belong—in the past where they happened. They don't spend much time pining for the good old days because they are too busy making new memories now. The negative pulls from the past are used not for self-flagellation or unproductive regret, but rather productive regret where they use lessons learned as stepping stones towards a better future.

4. Show me a positive person and I can show you a grateful person

The most positive people are the most grateful people. They do not focus on the potholes of their lives. They focus on the pot of gold that awaits them every day, with new smells, sights, feelings and experiences. They see life as a treasure chest full of wonder.

5. Rather than being stuck in their limitations, positive people are energized by their possibilities

Optimistic people focus on what they can do, not what they can't do. They are not fooled to think that there is a perfect solution to every problem, and are confident that there are many solutions and possibilities. They are not afraid to attempt new solutions to old problems, rather than spin their wheels expecting things to be different this time.

对于给我带来消极影响的人，我会保持距离，或者任由他们而去；

而且，我有分辨这两种人之间不同的智慧！

2. 乐观人群不仅会享受美好的一天——还会创造美好的一天

乐观人群的字典里很少会有“等待”、“希望”、“企盼”这样的词汇。反之，他们总是用那些强而有力、积极主动的字眼，而不会用那些被动的字眼。被动性会导致人缺乏参与精神，而乐观人群会积极参与到自己的人生规划中。在艰难时期，他们会用行动来改善自己的感受，而不是仅仅盼着坏情绪消失。

3. 对于乐观人群来说，过去只停留在过去

好的和坏的回忆都应该留在原地——也就是事情发生的过去。乐观人群不会花很多时间来怀念美好的旧时光，因为他们正忙着创造新的回忆。过去那些负面回忆不是用来让你自责不已的，也不是让你毫无意义地后悔，而是让你在后悔中吸取经验教训，然后让其成为走向更美好未来的垫脚石。

4. 乐观人群都是懂得感恩的人

最乐观的人往往也是最懂得感恩的人。他们不会揪着生活中的坎坷不放，而会用全新的感官和体验，去关注生活中每天都在等待着他们的宝藏。在他们眼中，生活就是一个充满了传奇的宝库。

5. 乐观人群不会为自己的局限所困，而会被自己的潜能所激励

乐观人群会关注自己所能做的，而不是他们所不能做的。他们不会愚钝地相信每个问题都会有完美的解决办法，他们只是确信每个问题都有许多解决办法和可能性。他们绝不会原地祈祷事情出现转机，而会毫无畏惧地尝试用新办法解决老问题。

6. Positive people do not let their fears interfere with their lives!

Positive people have observed that those who are defined and pulled back by their fears never really truly live a full life. While proceeding with appropriate caution, they do not let fear keep them from trying new things. They realize that even failures are necessary steps for a successful life. They have confidence that they can get back up when they are knocked down by life events or their own mistakes, due to a strong belief in their personal resilience.

7. Positive people smile a lot!

When you feel positive on the inside it is like you are smiling from within, and these smiles are contagious. Furthermore, the more others are with positive people, the more they tend to smile too! They see the lightness in life, and have a sense of humor even when it is about themselves. Positive people have a high degree of self-respect, but refuse to take themselves too seriously!

8. People who are positive are great communicators

They realize that assertive, confident communication is the only way to connect with others in everyday life. They avoid judgmental, angry interchanges, and do not let someone else's blow up give them a reason to react in kind. Rather, they express themselves with tact and finesse. They also refuse to be non-assertive and let people push them around. They refuse to own problems that belong to someone else.

9. Positive people realize that if you live long enough, there are times for great pain and sadness

One of the most common misperceptions about positive people is that to be positive, you must always be happy. This can not be further from the truth. Anyone who has any depth at all is certainly not happy all the time. Being sad, angry, disappointed are all essential emotions in life. How else would you ever

6. 乐观人群不会让恐惧妨碍他们的生活！

乐观人群明白，那些被恐惧所束缚和牵绊的人永远无法真正活出自己的人生。他们也会保持适当的谨慎，但不会让恐惧阻止他们对新事物的尝试。他们深知，失败也是通往成功的必经之路。他们坚信，哪怕被生活中的挫折或自己犯下的错误所打倒，他们也可以重新站起来，因为他们对于自己的复原能力有着强烈的信念。

7. 乐观人群常常微笑！

如果你感到积极乐观，你也会发自内心地微笑，而且这种微笑是具有传染性的。此外，和乐观人群相处越久的人，也就越容易微笑！乐观人群能够发现生活的闪光点，而且富有幽默感，即便是拿自己开玩笑也毫不介意。他们有很强的自尊，但不会把自己太当回事儿！

8. 乐观人群十分善于交流

乐观人群明白，积极自信的交流是日常生活中与他人沟通的唯一方式。他们会避免批判性的、愤怒的交谈，也不会因为他人出言不逊就以牙还牙。相反，他们在自我表达时善于运用机智和策略。他们还充满自信，绝不会任人摆布，也不会亦步亦趋地跟着别人犯错误。

9. 乐观人群明白，你活得越长，痛苦和悲伤也会越多

对乐观人群一个最常见的误解就是，他们每时每刻都是快乐的。这简直是大错特错。任何一个头脑正常的人都不可能永远快乐。悲伤、愤怒和失望也是生命中非常重要的情绪。如果你只拥有否定和肤浅的情绪，如何能做到对他人感同身受呢？乐观人群在面对各种情绪时不会逃避，他们认

develop empathy for others if you lived a life of denial and shallow emotions? Positive people do not run from the gamut of emotions, and accept that part of the healing process is to allow themselves to experience all types of feelings, not only the happy ones. A positive person always holds the hope that there is light at the end of the darkness.

10. Positive person are empowered people—they refuse to blame others and are not victims in life

Positive people seek the help and support of others who are supportive and safe. They have identified their own basic human rights, and they respect themselves too much to play the part of a victim. There is no place for holding grudges with a positive mindset. Forgiveness helps positive people become better, not bitter.

How about you? How many habits of positive people do you personally find in yourself? If you lack even a few of these 10 essential habits, you might find that the expected treasure at the end of the rainbow was not all that it was cracked up to be. How could it—if you keep on bringing a negative attitude around?

为情绪上的治愈过程会让他们体验多种情感，而不仅仅是快乐这一种。一个乐观的人总是相信，黑暗的尽头必有光明。

10. 乐观人群善于掌控自己的人生——他们不会责怪他人，也不会做生活的受害者

乐观人群会向有能力且可靠的人寻求帮助和支持。他们很明确自己的基本人权，而且非常维护自己的尊严，因此不会扮演受害者的角色。乐观人群拥有积极的心态，绝不会心存怨恨。宽容有助于乐观人群抛弃愁苦，让他们的生活变得更美好。

那么，你呢？你在自己身上找到了多少积极人群的习惯呢？如果你仅仅是缺乏这 10 种习惯中的几条，你可能就会发现，你所期待的彩虹尽头的宝藏也不像传说中的那样。它怎么可能如你所期——如果你还继续保持一种消极的态度？

The Gift of Possibility
送给自己的圣诞礼物

◎ Esmeralda Santiago

That Christmas Eve, the streets of Boston were clogged with tourists and locals bundled in wool and flannel. Shoppers, hawkers, and gawkers whirled and swirled around me. "Frosty the Snowman", "Let It Snow" and "Jingle Bells" played in stores; on the sidewalks, the street musicians did their best. Everyone, it seemed, was accompanied by someone else smiling or laughing. I was alone.

The eldest of a Puerto Rican family of 11 children growing up in New York's crowded tenements, I'd spent much of my life seeking solitude. Now, finally, at 27, a college student in the midst of a drawn-out breakup of a seven-year relationship, I contemplated what I'd so craved, but I wasn't quite sure I liked it. Every part of me wanted to be alone, but not at Christmas.

My family had returned to Puerto Rico, my friends had gone home during the holiday break, and my acquaintances were involved in their own lives. Dusk was falling, and the inevitable return to my empty apartment brought tears to my eyes. Blinking lights from windows and around doors beckoned, and I wished someone would emerge from one of those homes to ask me inside to a warm room with a Christmas tree decorated with tinsel, its velvet skirt sprinkled with shiny fake snow and wrapped presents.

名人语库

Life can only be understood backwards, but it must be lived forwards.

Kierkergaard

只有向后才能理解生活；但要生活好，则必须向前看。

克尔凯郭尔（丹麦哲学家）

那年圣诞前夕，波士顿的街道上满是熙熙攘攘的游客，当地人裹着羊毛和法兰绒打扮得光鲜靓丽。购物者、小贩和路人把我围在中间。商店里播放着《结霜的雪人》《下雪吧》和《铃儿响叮当》；人行道上，街头音乐家卖力地表演着。看起来似乎每个人都有人陪伴，脸上绽放出幸福的笑容。只有我是独自一人。

我家是一个波多黎各大家庭，一共有 11 个孩子，我是家里的长子，我们从小生活在纽约城拥挤的租住房里。在一生的大部分时间，我都在寻求片刻的孤独。此时此刻，终于，我这个 27 岁的大学生，结束了一段 7 年的漫长恋情，得到了我想要的孤独，可我却并不觉得开心。我想一个人静一静，但不是在圣诞节这样的日子。

我的家人已经回到了波多黎各，我的朋友都在假期回家了，我认识的人都忙于自己的生活。夜幕降临，想着还得回到那空荡荡的宿舍，眼泪就涌了出来。城市住家的灯火点亮起来，从门窗透出的闪烁灯光仿佛在召唤着我，我多希望有人会打开房门，邀请我走进那温暖的房间，房间一角是一株圣诞树，圣诞彩条将它装饰得绚烂华丽，天鹅绒的树摆上点缀着闪亮

I stopped at the local market, feeling even more depressed as people filled their baskets with goodies. Dates and dried figs, walnuts, pecans, and hazelnuts in their shells reminded me of the gifts we received as children in Puerto Rico on Christmas Day, because the big gifts were given on the morning of the Feast of the Epiphany, on January 6. I missed my family: their rambunctious parties; the dancing; the mounds of rice with pigeon peas; the crusty, garlicky skin on the pork roast; the plantain and yucca pasteles wrapped in banana leaves. I wanted to cry for wanting to be alone and for having achieved it.

In front of the church down the street, a manger had been set up, with Mary, Joseph, and the barn animals in expectation of midnight and the arrival of baby Jesus. I stood with my neighbors watching the scene, some of them crossing themselves, praying. As I walked home, I realized that the story of Joseph and Mary wandering from door to door seeking shelter was much like my own history. Leaving Puerto Rico was still a wound in my soul as I struggled with who I had become in 15 years in the United States. I'd mourned the losses, but for the first time, I recognized what I'd gained. I was independent, educated, healthy, and adventurous. My life was still before me, full of possibility.

Sometimes the best gift is the one you give yourself. That Christmas, I gave myself credit for what I'd accomplished so far and permission to go forward, unafraid. It is the best gift I've ever received, the one that I most treasure.

的人造雪花和包装好的礼物。

我在集市边停下脚步，看到人们提着装满美食的篮子，心中感到更加沮丧。椰枣、无花果干、核桃和山核桃，还有带壳的榛子，让我想起小时候在波多黎各收到的圣诞礼物——1 月 6 日主显节上午，我们才能收到圣诞大礼。我想念我的家人：想念他们喧闹的派对，想念他们多姿的舞蹈，想念香喷喷的木豆米饭，想念烤乳猪的蒜味脆皮，想念芭蕉叶包裹的大蕉丝兰根。我得到了我想要的孤独，却忍不住想哭。

在街道尽头的教堂前，布置好了一条马槽，玛丽、约瑟夫和马厩里的动物们都在期待着午夜到来，耶稣降临。我和邻居站在那里看着这幅场景，有些人手画十字、低头祈祷。在回家路上，我意识到，约瑟夫和玛丽挨家挨户寻求庇护的故事，就如同我自己的经历。离开波多黎各始终是我心头难以化解的伤痛，我一直在想，15 年的美国生活让我变成了一个什么样的人。我本应为我所失去的感到悲伤，但那一刻，我第一次认识到我获得了什么。我是一个独立的、受过良好教育的、健康的、富有冒险精神的青年。我的生活就在我的面前，充满了无尽的可能性。

有时候，你送给自己的礼物才是最好的礼物。那年圣诞节，我送给自己的是肯定和许诺，肯定自己过去的努力，许诺自己奋勇向前，无所畏惧。这是我收到的最好的礼物，我最珍惜的圣诞礼物。

Think About This

15句最暖心的话

◎ Anonymous

1. At least 2 people in this world love you so much they would die for you.

2. At least 15 people in this world love you in some way.

3. The only reason anyone would ever hate you is because they want to be just like you.

4. A smile from you can bring happiness to anyone, even if they don't like you.

5. Every night, someone thinks about you before they go to sleep.

6. You mean the world to someone.

7. If not for you, someone may not be living.

8. You are special and unique.

9. Someone that you don't even know exists, loves you.

10. When you make the biggest mistake ever, something good always comes from it.

11. When you think the world has turned its back on you, take a look: you most likely turned your back on the world.

12. When you think you have no chance of getting what you want, you probably won't get it, but if you believe in yourself, probably, sooner or later,

名人语库

Happiness is a perfume you cannot pour on others without getting a few drops on yourself.

Ralph Waldo Emerson

幸福犹如香水，在你将它洒向别人的时候，自己也会沾染点滴。

拉尔夫·沃尔多·爱默生（美国思想家、诗人）

1. 在这个世界上至少有 2 个人很爱你，他们愿意为你而死。

2. 在这个世界上至少有 15 个人以某种方式爱着你。

3. 有人会恨你的唯一原因就是因为他们想变得和你一样。

4. 你的微笑可以给每一个人带来快乐，即使他们不喜欢你。

5. 每个夜晚，都有人会在入睡前想着你。

6. 对某个人来说，你就是全世界。

7. 如果不是因为你，某个人可能活不下去。

8. 你是独一无二的。

9. 有人爱着你，而你甚至都不知道他的存在。

10. 当你犯了天大的错误时，总有一些好事及时到来。

11. 如果你认为全世界都背弃了你，好好看看：最有可能的是你背弃了全世界。

12. 当你认为你没机会得到你想要的东西时，你可能得不到它，但如果你相信自己，也许迟早你都会得到它。

you will get it.

13. Always remember the compliments you received. Forget about the rude remarks.

14. Always tell someone how you feel about them; you will feel much better when they know.

15. If you have a great friend, take the time to let them know that they are great before it's too late.

13. 永远记住你所收获的赞美。忘掉那些粗鲁的言语。

14. 要告诉别人你对他们的感觉；当他们了解以后，你会感觉更棒。

15. 如果你有很棒的朋友，花点时间让他们知道他们有多棒——趁一切还来得及。

Everybody Has a Dream

每个人都有梦想

◎ Virginia Satir

Some years ago I took on an assignment in a southern county to work with people on public welfare. What I wanted to do was show that everybody has the capacity to be self-sufficient and all we have to do is to activate them. I asked the county to pick a group of people who were on public welfare, people from different racial groups and different family constellations. I would then see them as a group for three hours every Friday. I also asked for a little petty cash to work with, as I needed it.

The first thing I said after I shook hands with everybody was, "I would like to know what your dreams are." Everyone looked at me as if I were kind of wacky.

"Dreams? We don't have dreams."

I said, "Well, when you were a kid what happened? Wasn't there something you wanted to do?"

One woman said to me, "I don't know what you can do with dreams. The rats are eating up my kids."

"Oh," I said. "That's terrible. No, of course, you are very much involved with the rats and your kids. How can that be helped?"

名人语库

No man is useless in this world who lightens the burden of someone else.

C. Dickens

在这个世界上能为别人减轻负担的人都是有用的。

查尔斯·狄更斯（英国小说家）

几年前，我被派遣到南部的一个镇上去指导依靠公共福利生活的人。我想做的就是告诉每个人，他们都有自给自足的能力，我们要做的就是激励他们。我让镇里挑选一批靠公共福利生活的人，他们应来自不同的种族和不同的家庭出身。然后，我会在每星期五与这些人待上三个小时。我还申请了一小笔工作资金，以备不时之需。

在同每个人一一握手之后，我说的第一句话就是："我想知道你们的梦想都是什么。"每个人都用异样的眼光看着我，好像我是一个怪人。

"梦想？我们没有梦想。"

我说："好吧，当你们还是个孩子的时候呢？你们没有什么想做的事吗？"

一位女士对我说："我不知道有了梦想又能做什么。老鼠就要吃掉我的孩子了。"

"哦，"我说，"那可真糟糕。你老是想着老鼠和你的孩子，那梦想当然没什么用。怎样才能帮到你呢？"

"Well, I could use a new screen door because there are holes in my screen door."

I asked, "Is there anybody around here who knows how to fix a screen door?"

There was a man in the group, and he said, "A long time ago I used to do things like that but now I have a terribly bad back, but I'll try."

I told him I had some money if he would go to the store and buy some screening and go and fix the lady's screen door.

"Do you think you can do that?"

"Yes, I'll try."

The next week, when the group was seated, I said to the woman, "Well, is your screen door fixed?"

"Oh, yes," she said.

"Then we can start dreaming, can't we?" She sort of smiled at me.

I said to the man who did the work, "How do you feel?"

He said, "Well, you know, it's a very funny thing. I'm beginning to feel a lot better."

That helped the group to begin to dream. These seemingly small successes allowed the group to see that dreams were not insane. These small steps began to get people to see and feel that something really could happen.

I began to ask other people about their dreams. One woman shared that she always wanted to be a secretary. I said, "Well, what stands in your way?"(That's always my next question.)

She said, "I have six kids, and I don't have anyone to take care of them while I'm away."

"Let's find out," I said.

“嗯……我也许需要一扇新的纱门，我的纱门洞太多了。”

我问：“这里有没有谁知道怎么安装纱门？”

这时，人群里有个男人说道：“很久以前，我常做那样的工作，但现在我的背痛得厉害，不过我会试试。”

我告诉他我有些钱，问他能否去商店买些网眼纱，然后去帮那位女士安装纱门。

“你认为你能做到这些吗？”

“是的，我试试。”

一周以后，当小组成员都坐好后，我对那位女士说：“好吧，你的纱门安装好了吗？”

“哦，是的。”她说。

“那么我们可以开始梦想了，不是吗？”她对我笑了笑。

我对那个安装纱门的男人说：“你感觉如何？”

他说：“噢，你知道，这是件很有趣的事。我现在感觉好多了。”

这件事使得整组人开始梦想起来。这些看似微不足道的成功让他们领会到，梦想并不愚蠢。这些小小的步骤开始让人们看见并感受到，有些事情真的会发生。

我开始询问其他人的梦想。一位女士分享道，她一直想做一个秘书。我说：“嗯，那么是什么阻碍了你的梦想呢？”（这总是我下一个要问的问题。）

她说：“我有六个孩子，当我外出的时侯，我找不到人去照顾他们。”

“让我们来看看有没有办法。”我说。

“这位女士每周在社区大学接受培训的一两天里，这个小组里有人能照

"Is there anybody in this group who would take care of six kids for a day or two a week while this woman gets some training here at the community college?"

One woman said, "I got kids, too, but I could do that."

"Let's do it," I said. So a plan was created and the woman went to school.

Everyone found something. The man who put in the screen door became a handyman. The woman who took in the children became a licensed foster care person. In 12 weeks I had all these people off public welfare. I've not only done that once, I've done in many times.

顾一下她的六个孩子吗？”

一位女士说道：“我也有孩子，但我可以帮忙。”

“那就这么办。”我说。于是一个计划出炉了，那位女士去上课了。

每个人都有所领悟。那位安装纱门的男人成了一名杂务工。这位帮忙照看孩子的女人成了一名有执照的看护师。十二周后，我使得这组人都不再依靠公共福利而生活。这样的事，我不仅只成功了一次，而是已经帮助了更多的人自食其力。

Growth From Discontent: Life's Way of Giving You a Little Push

学会在不满意中成长

◎ Edward B. Toupin

That strange, gut-wrenching feeling you have is not the sushi you had for lunch. It's your soul trying to give you a nudge to do something. A word for that feeling is "discontent". Discontent is a state of not being satisfied or fulfilled in your current situation.

Of course, this same feeling can apply to a hundred different situations, from a work-related issue to a personal issue at home. But, the resulting meaning is still the same: "make a change." Some people listen to that feeling and change their life in such a way as to eliminate that feeling. However, some people that fall into discontent, but tend to remain in that situation as they find it a place of "same-ness" and "safety".

Souler Greenhouse

Discontent is actually a "souler greenhouse" of change. It is the first warnings you receive that things are not what they should be and that a change is required to correct the situation. Discontent comes when there is juxtaposition between needs and desires. Usually, you're pursuing a need, achieve it, and then continue to pursue the ideals of the same need. This occurs because you don't know what to do once you reach the objective. However, once you achieve a

名人语库

A thought which does not result in an action is nothing much, and an action which does not proceed from a thought is nothing at all.

Georges Bernanos

思想倘若不引发行动则意义不大，而行动倘若不是源于思想则毫无意义。

乔治斯·贝尔纳诺斯（法国作家）

那个奇怪、挠心的感觉并不是因为你午饭吃的寿司。那是你的灵魂给你一个动力要让你去做某件事。用一个词来概括这种感觉，就是“不满”。不满是对你现状的不满意或不满足。

当然，这同样的感觉也能出现在各种各样的情况下，从工作事宜到家庭个人问题。但是，由此而来的意义都一样：“要做出改变。”有些人会倾听这种感觉，然后去改变他们的生活以消除这种感觉。然而，另一些人会陷入这种不满当中，他们往往只是持续这种状况，因为他们感觉在其中“一样”和“安全”。

灵魂温室

不满实际上是一个变相的“灵魂温室”。它是当事情不是应该的样子、需要改变纠正情况时，发给你的最初的警告。当需求和渴求并列出现时，不满就会现身。通常，你在追求一个需求，实现了，然后继续追求同样的需求。之所以会出现这种情况，是因为你不知道达到目标后该做什么。然而，一旦你实现了需求，你就需要继续下一个追求。

need, you need to move on to the next pursuit.

Many people find that discontent for a given situation is acceptable. For instance, discontent with your work might feel acceptable because you have to make money and care for your family. In this way, you learn to overcome the discontent by accepting the obligations. However, while this may work, it is not necessarily the route to take. Indeed, you might need the job, but this feeling is calling for an evaluation as some aspect of the situation needs attention.

Discontent can provide you with either a reason to stay right where you are or a fertile environment from which to move forward. While it does provide a way for the universe to bring attention to a situation, we sometimes become so accustomed to the feeling that it becomes part of our life. In such a case, if we adapt and the discontented feeling is resolved, we will miss it.

Growth

Growth from discontent is an amazing change. Again, comparing to the greenhouse, it can either smother you, or help you grow. However, change from discontent is something that you have to execute consciously, because discontent can also provide you with a safety zone. By accepting discontent in one part of your life, it can spread into other areas of your life. You can become satisfied with the feeling because it becomes familiar. However, you end up working on parts of your life in hopes of resolving the feeling when you find that, once that part of your life has changed, you still feel the same.

Growth occurs because you feel a push, or pull, to move in a direction. The objective is to obtain a balance such that the discontent disappears. Once you achieve the necessary change, you will be able to leave the discontented feelings behind you. Focus on the situation that makes you feel the discontent, not on

许多人认为对某个处境不满是可以接受的。例如，对工作不满可以让人接受，因为你必须赚钱养家。这样，你学会了通过接受义务来克服不满。然而，尽管这也许奏效，却不一定是一条必选之路。的确，你可能需要这份工作，但是这种感觉是要求你对此作出评估，因为这个处境下的某个方面需要考虑。

不满提供给你的，要么是一个呆在原地的理由，要么是一个奋勇直前的丰硕环境。虽然它确实让人们关注一个处境，但是有时候我们对于这种感觉过于习以为常，因此它已经成为了我们生活的一部分。在这种情况下，如果我们适应了，而不满感也被解决，那么我们就会失去它。

成长

从不满中成长是一个令人惊奇的改变。同样用温室来比较，它可以令你窒息，又可以帮助你成长。然而，不满带来何种改变是要你有意识去执行的，因为不满还能为你提供一个舒适区。若你已接受生活中的一部分不满，不满就会漫及到你生活中的其他方方面面。你可能会对不满的感觉一直感到“满意”，因为它已经变得熟悉。然而，最终你会从生活各个部分去努力解决这种感觉，此时你就会发现当生活的某部分已经改变了，你却还是同样的感受。

当你感觉到朝着某个方向有一个推力或拉力时，你就会成长。目标是要获得一种平衡，这样不满就会消失。一旦你达到必要的改变，你将能把不满情绪抛在身后。关注于让你感觉不满的处境，而不是其他可能或可能不会让你感觉更好的问题上。从“忙于工作”、修理某样没坏的东西中获得

other issues that may, or may not, make you feel better. The contented feeling from "doing busy work" or fixing something that isn't broken is fleeting, unless you tackle the core issue.

The growth comes in once you embrace the change. When you move from an area of the familiar, you must learn something new or different to adapt to the unfamiliar. However, in this transition, you are putting your life back in balance and moving forward, which eliminates those feelings of discontent.

What's next?

Don't let discontent drag you down! Listen to your gut! It will always tell you when change is necessary. It might be a simple gnawing feeling or a twisted knot. In either case, be honest with yourself and trust that feeling. Discontent is the universe's way of telling you that a change is necessary within yourself to resolve the situation. It is there to warn you of situations and guide you when things need to change.

To make the change, you have to know where you are and where you want to be in the near future. However, the one thing to keep in mind is that you want to achieve some type of balance to counter the discontent. Remember that discontent is caused from an imbalance in one or more parts of your life. Ask yourself, and focus on, what it is that is causing you the most concern. Once you are able to determine the issue, only then can you set out on a goal that satisfies the feeling. Such an approach will not only restore balance, but it will also allow you to move forward to a more fulfilling life.

的满足感，这是转瞬即逝的，除非你能解决核心问题。

一旦你成功改变，你也就成长了。当你从一个熟悉的领域走出来时，你必须学习新的或不同的东西来适应陌生感。不过，在这个转变过程中，你会重新让生活恢复平衡，并且向前进，这样就能把不满感消除。

下一步呢?

不要让不满拖后腿！听从你的心声！它总会告诉你何时有必要作出改变了。这可能只是一般的痛苦或纠结。不论怎样，对自己诚实，并相信这种感觉。不满是自然在告诉你，你必须要做出改变来解决目前的问题。它是要对你的处境发出警报，引导你做出所需的改变。

想要作出改变，你必须了解你目前的状况，以及不远将来的预想状况。然而，要记住一点，你希望用某种平衡来抵制不满。记住，不满是由于生活中一个或多个部分失衡所引起的。问一问自己，集中精力，什么是你最关心的。一旦你确定了问题所在，你才能开始制定一个满足自己的目标。这个方法不但能恢复平衡，还能让你朝更满意的生活前进。

记忆永恒，寂寞也美

Don't forget the things you once owned. Treasure the things you can't get. Don't give up the things that belong to you and keep those lost things in memory.

曾经拥有的，不要忘记。不能得到的，更要珍惜。属于自己的，不要放弃。已经失去的，留作回忆。

Let the Candle Relight
别让蜡烛熄灭

◎ Anonymous

A man had a little daughter—an only and much-loved child. He lived for her—she was his life. So when she became ill, he became like a man possessed, moving heaven and earth to bring about her restoration to health.

His best efforts, however, proved unavailing and the child died. The father became a bitter recluse, shutting himself away from his many friends and refusing every activity that might restore his poise and bring him back to his normal self. But one night he had a dream.

He was in heaven, witnessing a grand pageant of all the little child angels. They were marching in a line passing by the Great White Throne. Every white-robed angelic child carried a candle. He noticed that one child's candle was not lighted. Then he saw that the child with the dark candle was his own little girl. Rushing to her, he seized her in his arms, caressed her tenderly, and then asked, "How is it, darling, that your candle alone is unlighted?"

"Daddy, they often relight it, but your tears always put it out."

Just then he awoke from his dream. The lesson was crystal clear, and its effects were immediate. From that hour on he was not a recluse, but mingled freely and cheerfully with his former friends and associates. No longer would his darling's candle be extinguished by his useless tears.

Don't cry because it is over, smile because it happened.

名人语库

There is no such thing as darkness; only a failure to see.

Malcolm Muggeridge

没有黑暗这种东西，只有看不见而已。

马尔科姆·马格里奇（英国作家、记者）

一个男人有一个小女儿——他唯一的、深深爱着的孩子。他为了她而活着——她是他的整个生命。所以，当女儿生病时，他像疯了似的竭尽全力想让她恢复健康。

他尽了最大的努力，但是一切都无济于事，女儿还是死了。父亲变得痛苦遁世，远离了许多朋友，拒绝参加一切能使他恢复平静、回到正常自我的活动。然而有一天晚上，他做了一个梦。

他来到了天堂，看到了一场盛大的小天使盛会。他们走成一条直线，经过白色大宝座。每个白衣小天使都拿着一支蜡烛。他注意到，有一个小天使的蜡烛没有点亮。然后，他看到那个蜡烛灭了的小女孩正是他的女儿。他冲过去，一把把她搂在怀里，温柔地抚摸着她，然后问道："亲爱的，怎么会这样，只有你的蜡烛没有点亮？"

"爸爸，他们经常重新点亮它，只是你的眼泪总是把它熄灭。"

就在这时，他从梦中醒来。这一课的启发是显而易见的，而且立竿见影。从那个时刻起，他不再把自己封闭起来，而是自由自在、轻松愉快地回到他从前的朋友和同事中间。宝贝女儿的蜡烛再也没有被他无用的泪水熄灭过。

不要因为结束而哭泣，微笑吧，为你的曾经拥有。

Sometimes Happiness Requires Nail Holes in Life
记忆留痕

◎ Roger Dean Kiser

Finally, for the first time in my life, I was going to move into brand-new house and it was an absolute beauty.

I spent hours upon hours walking up and down the hallway just looking at that sunken living room. I had never actually seen one of those before and always thought they were only for rich people. It sure made me proud to now have one for my very own. I smiled real big and then put a foot down onto the first step, which led down onto the beautifully carpeted living room. Then I carefully looked to make sure I did not get any dirt on the golden colored carpet. Then I removed my shoes and walked all around the living room, feeling the soft, new, thick carpet beneath my feet.

I met the real estate agent for the last time, signed the final papers and he handed me the keys. I jumped into my car and rushed as fast as I could to my rented mobile home to get the family and start the moving-in process. That was a very good day in my life, because no one in my family would ever have to live on the streets like I did as a young boy when running away from that abusive Florida orphanage. This house would be kept in brand-new condition, and would last forever and ever—so that all my children, grandchildren and great

名人语库

Life is ten percent what you make it and ninety percent how you take it.

Irving Berlin

生活有百分之十在于你如何塑造它，有百分之九十在于你如何对待它。

欧文·柏林（美国作曲家）

终于，我人生中第一次即将要搬进新家，这所房子绝对称得上美妙至极。

我来来回回地在走廊上溜达了几个小时，就为了观看那沉降式的客厅。我以前从没见过这些，也总认为那只是属于有钱人的。现在，我真的感到自豪，因为我也拥有了这样一个客厅。我笑容满面，伸出一只脚踏在第一级台阶上，台阶下面是铺着精美地毯的客厅。我小心翼翼地观看着，确保我没有把一丁点尘土留在金色的地毯上。然后我脱掉了鞋子，在客厅里来回地走，尽情感受着脚底下那柔软、厚实的新地毯。

我与房地产经纪人见了最后一次面，签署了最终的文件后，他把房子钥匙递给了我。我跳进车里，用我最快的速度驶到我租来的房屋，去那里接我的家人，并开始着手搬家。 这是我生命中特别美好的一天，因为从此以后，我的家人再也不会像童年的我那样流落街头——小时候，我在逃离那个备受虐待的佛罗里达孤儿院后，就住在大街上。我要让这所房子始终保持崭新的状态，让它永久长存——这样一来，不管怎样我所有的孙子和曾孙们，就可以一直住在一个崭新而漂亮的地方。

grandchildren would always have a nice, new looking place to live, no matter what.

That held true year after year and about five years later, we sold that immaculate house for top dollar. There was not a spot or smear or hole anywhere in that beautiful house. Not even on the walls could you find a small nail hole that would have held a picture. I was supposed to meet with the real estate agent who was selling our house later that evening and when I arrived, I was surprised to find the new owners of the house standing in the driveway. I parked my car, walked up and began talking with the older couple.

"This house is in perfect condition," said the old man.

"Perfect in every way. Not even a nail hole in any of the wall." I told him proudly.

"It's really too bad that nobody lived here," said the old woman.

"I lived here for five whole years." I said with a great big smile on my face.

"No. You didn't live here for five years. You just stayed here for five years." said the old lady.

All the way home I thought about what she said. What did she mean? How could they not be happy about buying a house in perfect condition and without any holes in the walls? I was very puzzled. Then it hit me like a ton of bricks. I quickly pulled over to the side of the road and just sat there thinking. The old lady was absolutely right.

Just because you stay in a house, it doesn't mean you really lived in it. Not unless you put your heart into it, enjoy it and do the things that make you happy while you are there—like walking into the living room and seeing pictures of the kids and the smiling faces of the grandchildren or watching them yelling their little lungs out under the sprinkler in your front yard, and yes maybe even a

年复一年，事情就如我想象中一样发展着。大约五年后，我们以最高的价格卖掉了这所完美的房子。这所美丽的房子里没有留下任何一处斑点、污渍或是小洞，甚至你在墙上也找不到一个曾因为挂画而留下的小钉孔！那晚稍晚些时候，我约了正在帮我们卖房子的房地产经纪人见面，当我到达的时候，惊讶地发现这所房子的新主人正站在车道上。我停下车子，走上前去，开始和这对老夫妇攀谈起来。

“这所房子堪称完美。”老先生说。

“一切都非常完美。甚至连任何一面墙上都找不到一个钉孔。”我很自豪地告诉他。

“这真是太糟糕了，没有人住过！”老太太说。

“我在这里住了整整五年呢。”我大笑着告诉她。

“不，你并没有在这里‘住’了五年，你只是在这里‘待’了五年而已。”老太太回应道。

回家的路上，我一直在思索着老太太的话。她说的是什么意思呢？他们能买到条件如此完美、墙上连一个小洞都没有的房子，怎么可能不高兴呢？我百思不得其解。突然，答案像砖头一样砸醒了我。我赶紧把车停在路边，坐在那里思考起来。老太太的话是完全正确的！

仅仅因为你搬进了一所房子里，并不意味着你真正在那里安家。除非你住在房子里的时候，全身心投入、乐在其中，并做着令自己快乐的事情——比如，走进客厅，看看墙上那些记录着子女孙辈们灿烂笑容的照片，或者看看他们在前院的喷水头下扯着嗓子大喊的照片，甚至还可以看看一张老狗在那美丽的地毯上撒尿的照片。

picture of the old dog who decided to go to the bathroom on that beautiful carpet.

I sat there alone biting my bottom lip and feeling very much ashamed of what I had done by having lost five years of my life, not to mention what I had taken from my family without even realizing it. Living really is much more than just remembering yesterday with only your mind. It is walking into your home and living for today with your heart and your eyes. Those holes in the wall, when all the furniture is gone and the house is completely bare, are memory holes and without any memories "You didn't really live there. You just stayed there."

Today, our home in Brunswick, Georgia has so many darn pictures of kid, grandkid, friends and dogs on the walls that it might collapse one day. And if it does that will be very sad for me. But today I'm living a happy life with everything around me.

我独自坐在那里，紧咬着下唇，感到很惭愧，我浪费了生命中的五年时光，更不用说我从家人那里剥夺了许多快乐，而自己却根本没意识到。生活，不仅仅意味着将昨日的印记留在脑海里，还意味着走进家里，用你的真心、你的双眼度过每一个今天。有一天，当所有的家具都移走了，这所房子也变得空荡荡时，房子墙上的那些孔洞就是记忆的痕迹。没有任何记忆，那就会像老太太所说的“你并不曾真正‘住’在那里，你只是在那里‘待’过而已。”

现在，我们的新家位于佐治亚州的不伦瑞克。家里的墙上挂满了照片，有子女们的、孙辈的、朋友的，还有小狗的，我真担心钉了那么多钉子后，墙壁也许有一天会坍塌。如果真的发生那样的事，我会非常伤心的。但是现在，我和我身边的所有人都过得非常快乐。

Loneliness

寂寞也美

◎ Deepak Chandrasekaren

"A man is known by the company he keeps." If it is so, then everyone is bound to have their baggage of loneliness with them as companions. Loneliness is not something that doesn't exist at all with any human being on earth. Every human being feels lonely in his life at some point or other. It's but natural to have such feeling, because that's what makes us all human and that is why we are as we are now.

If we shed some light on why we feel aloof or lonely at times, we would be very much astonished or even probably surprised by the results. We ourselves are responsible for our self-defined gloominess. This is because at times we really feel that we are un-cared for or feel someone doesn't understand us.

Sometimes we over analyze real life situations and have this growing sense of self pity inside us. This feeling always gives us thoughts which picturise us always receiving the wrong end of the stick in life. The truth might not always be true if we touch our heart and see. It's just that our expectations in life and from people around us or circumstances that we are facing have got the better of us. Expectation is the silent killer which murders millions of mushy and time tested relationships. If there would have been no expectations from anyone, the

名人语库

The main dangers in this life are the people who want to change everything—or nothing.

Lady Astor

生活中的主要危险来自那些想要改变一切或什么也不想改变的人。

阿斯特子爵夫人（英国下院第一位女议员）

“观其友，知其人。”如果的确如此，那么每个人都注定要与孤独为伴。在这个世界上，孤独感与每个人相生相伴。人们都会在某些特定的时刻感到孤独。这是十分自然的感觉，因为孤独感使我们成为人，并让我们成为现在的自己。

如果我们要阐明为什么有时会感到冷漠或孤独，我们会对得出的结果感到十分吃惊。我们应该对我们自定义的忧郁负责。这是因为，在有些时候，我们真的觉得自己被忽视或不被理解。

有时候我们过度地分析了自己的真实生活状况，这令我们在内心产生了一种自我怜悯的感觉。这种感觉经常会带给我们一种生活的错觉。如果我们扪心自问，真相并不总是真实的，它只是我们对于身边的人和环境过高的期待。期待是一个沉默的杀手，谋杀了无数亲密的、经过时间考验的关系。如果我们不再总是对他人抱有期待，这个世界将会变得更好。如果不再有那么多期待，就不会有那么多人感到心痛，而对于有些人，一生也

world would have been a much better place to be. If there would have been no expectations, not many people would have had an aching heart and a life long grouse against there would have been better haves. If it wouldn't have been for unreasonable expectations not many couples would have divorced each other.

How to come out of expectations then? Good question. The answer is when you give something, don't always expect anything in return. When our mother gave birth to us, she never expected that we will give birth to her. She has just fulfilled her desire to raise a family and live for them. In the same way, let our actions make us live for our self and let not expectation screw up the major portion of your lives. Let us have the freedom and will power to express our love, affection and longingness for people whenever we feel. Let us not restrict our freedom of expression just because he or she is not responding the way we want them to.

Well, all in all a little bit of loneliness is good for a self-analysis to keep a check over your actions. Introspection always makes you communicate with the inner self, but too much of introspection can make you scale the altitude of self pity. So show restrain at the right time.

就不会有那么长的埋怨了。如果没有那些不合理的期待，也就不会有那么多夫妻离婚了。

那么怎样才能跳出期待呢？问得好。答案是，当我们给予的时候，不要总是期待有所回报。当我们的妈妈给予我们生命时，她从没有期望我们也给予她生命。她仅仅是完成了她拥有一个家庭并为之而活的理想。同样，让我们为自己而活，不要让期待占据你生命中的一大部分。让我们自由地、大声地表达我们的爱、感动和渴望。当别人没有像我们期待的那样回应时，我们也不要失去表达感情的自由。

当然，总的来说，一点点的孤独对一个人审视自己的行为是有好处的。自省总是会让你与你的心灵有所交流，但是过度的自省会使我们产生高度的自我怜悯感。因此，适当克制自己，要适而可止。

The Instant Beauty
瞬间之美

◎ Craig Wilson

My morning routine varies little from day to day. I walk the dog, eat breakfast at the kitchen counter with Katie and Matt, then settle in for a day at the computer.

And because I work mostly from home, I have learned that little forays into the outside world are imperative for psychological well-being.

So before I begin attempting to put sentences together, I stroll over to a quirky little coffee shop in my neighborhood, chat with the folks behind the counter, and get a large coffee to go. No sugar. No cream.

The coffee shop is on the other side of the historic Chesapeake & Ohio Canal from my house. In season, a mule-drawn barge is docked there, and tourists line up to take a slow boat, if not to Ancient China, at least into the 19th century.

The men who work the boat wear what canal workers might have worn back then—broad-brimmed straw hats and suspenders that pull their scratchy-looking pants high above their boots.

One warm day last fall, I was on my morning outing when I turned the corner to see one of the men sitting alone on the boat, bathed in early-morning

名人语库

Human felicity is produced not so much by great pieces of good fortune that seldom happen, as by little advantages that occur every day.

Benjamin Franklin

与其说人类的幸福来自偶尔发生的鸿运，不如说来自每天都有的小实惠。

本杰明·富兰克林（美国总统）

每天上午，我都要做这几件例行小事：带着小狗散步，在厨房餐桌前陪凯蒂和马特吃早餐，然后一头扎进电脑中开始一天的工作。

我主要在家里工作，但我明白，时不时到外面的世界闯荡一下，对保持良好的心态是必不可少的。

所以，在我推敲语句、下笔成文之前，我会漫步前往附近一间奇特的小咖啡店去，和店里的朋友们在柜台后聊聊天，然后带走一大杯咖啡——不加糖，不加奶。

我家不远处就是历史悠久的切撒皮克·俄亥俄运河，那间小咖啡店就坐落在运河的另一边。每到旺季时，就有一条骡子拉着驳船停靠在河岸边，游客们排着队等着乘坐一艘慢悠悠的船，即使不像是驶往古老的中国，至少也像是驶往 19 世纪的往日时光。

船上的工人穿着只有当年运河工人们才有的衣装：宽边草帽和吊带裤，吊带把他们那粗糙的裤子拉起来，露出靴子。

去年秋天一个暖和的早上，我像往日一样外出散步。转过街角时，我看到一个人静静地独自坐在一艘船上，沐浴在一片晨曦之中。

light.

He was playing a tiny accordion, the kind such canal men squeezed as they floated down the inland waterways of a westward-expanding America. The sound was both melancholy and sweet. It was as if he were alone in the universe.

The scene stopped me in my tracks. What I witnessed could only be described as a perfect moment. Ten seconds at most. But months later I still remember just standing there, watching, listening, taking it all in.

We all have such moments put before us. Little surprises. Whether we're wise enough to see them is another thing.

I thought of the accordion man Sunday afternoon while reading the biographies of those killed in the Columbia tragedy. Mission specialist Laurel Clark, talking from the shuttle a few days before it was to land, said she was delighted by the simple unexpected wonders of space. Like a sunset.

"There's a flash; the whole payload bay turns this rosy pink," she said. "It only lasts about 15 second and then it's gone. It's very ethereal and extremely beautiful."

A moment not lost on her.

In The Hours, Meryl Streep and Ed Harris recall a moment they shared years before at a beach house on Cape Cod. It was nothing more than him watching her walk out into the early-morning light. But for that moment, everything was right with their world, everything was possible, everything aligned. They agreed it was the happiest they had ever been.

And in last month's issue of her magazine, Oprah Winfrey confessed to a "moment" she had last summer. It was a walk down a Santa Barbara lane, a hummingbird and the smell of orange blossoms. She said it was one of those rare times she could say she was truly happy.

他在船上拉着一个小小的手风琴，正如当年的运河船工一样，抚琴驾舟，沿着这条古老的内陆河道驶往美国西部。琴声忧郁而甜美。仿佛整个宇宙都只有他一个人。

这番美景让我不禁停下了脚步。我所看到的一切，只能用完美时刻来形容。这最多只有十秒的时光。但是几个月后，我还清晰地记得当时我只是站在那儿，静静地注视着，倾听着，把所有的景象都印入脑海里。

我们都曾经历过这样的时刻。小小的惊喜。然而，我们能否拥有发现这种美的智慧，就是另一回事了。

一个周日的下午，当我阅读在哥伦比亚号航天飞机事故中丧生的宇航员的传记时，我又想起了那个拉手风琴的人。执行航天任务的女专家劳雷尔·克拉克，在飞机着陆前的几天曾说过，她能看见太空中那些意想不到的美景奇观，这让她十分开心。比如日落。

“有一道闪光；整个有效载荷舱都被晕染成了这种玫瑰红，”她说，“仅仅持续了 15 秒便消失了。这过程神奇且美轮美奂。”

她没有错过这一瞬间。

在电影《时时刻刻》里，梅丽尔·斯特里普和埃德·哈里斯回忆起多年前他们在科德角上的沙滩小屋共度的时光。就是他看着她走进晨曦的那一幕。就在那一刻，在他们的二人世界里，一切都刚刚好，一切都变得可能。他们认为，那是他们一生中最幸福的时刻。

奥普拉·温弗瑞在她上个月出刊的杂志中提到，去年夏天她也有过一次“美妙时刻”。那一刻她正走在圣巴巴拉市的一条小巷子里，突然看见一只蜂鸟，和着一阵扑面而来的橘子花香。她说，这是她一生中难得几次真正感到幸福的时刻之一。

I once had a friend who had an odd habit that never ceased to amuse me, maybe because I never quite knew when she was going to spring it on me.

It could be while sitting quietly at the end of a dock on Schroon Lake in the Adirondacks. Or it could come in the middle of a particularly lively dinner with old friends.

Out of the blue, she'd say, "Stop! I want to remember this moment."

I realize now, after her death, what wise advice that is.

我有个朋友，她有个古怪的习惯，总是让我觉得很好笑，也许是因为我永远都不知道她的怪癖将在何时又逗我开心。

或许在我们静静地坐在阿迪朗达克山下舒伦湖边的码头边上之时，或许在和老朋友那次十分热闹的聚餐之时。

每在这样的时刻，她都会突然说："停！我要记住这一刻！"

后来在她去世后，我终于意识到，那是多么智慧的言语。

Discovery in a Thunderstorm

雷雨中的醒悟

◎ Dr. Nelson Glueck

Many years ago I was on a bicycle trip through some exceedingly picturesque countryside. Suddenly, dark clouds piled up overhead and rain began to fall, but strange to relate, several hundred yards ahead of me the sun shone brilliantly. Pedaling, however, as rapidly as I could, I found it impossible to get into the clear. The clouds with their rain kept advancing faster than I could race forward. I continued this unequal contest for an exhausting half hour, before realizing that I could not win my way to the bright area ahead of me.

Then it dawned upon me that I was wasting my strength in unimportant hurry, while paying no attention whatsoever to the landscape for the sake of which I was making the trip. The storm could not last forever and the discomfort was not unendurable. Indeed, there was much to look at which might otherwise have escaped me. As I gazed about with sharpened appreciation, I saw colors and lines and contours that would have appeared differently under brilliant light. The rain mists which now crowned the wooded hills and the fresh clearness of the different greens were entrancing. My annoyance at the rain was gone and my eagerness to escape it vanished. It had provided me with a new view and helped me understand that the sources of beauty and satisfaction may be found close at

名人语库

Every soil where he is well, is to a valiant man his natural country.

Masinger Phililp

勇敢的人随遇而安，所到之处都是故乡。

菲利普·马新杰（英国剧作家）

许多年前，我曾骑着自行车从一片风景如画的郊野中穿过。突然，乌云密布，大雨滂沱，然而奇怪的是，在前方几百码的地方却是阳光灿烂。我使劲地蹬着踏板往前冲，却发现怎么也到不了那片阳光普照之地。乌云夹着大雨，总是赶在我的前面。半小时后，我累得筋疲力尽，停止了这场不公平的竞赛，才意识到自己根本无法抵达那片明朗天地。

顿时，我豁然开朗，我是在无关紧要的事情上浪费力气，匆忙奔波，却忽略了途中的景致，忘记了旅行的目的。暴风雨不会永不停息，任何不适也并非无法容忍。事实上，我差点错过了途中那无尽的美好景致。我满怀感激地凝视着眼前的景色，我所看见的色彩、线条和轮廓，比起在阳光下则另有一番风味。繁茂的山林烟雨朦胧，别样的绿树清新明朗，令人神迷。大雨带给我的烦恼瞬间消散，渴望逃离的欲望也不复存在。它带给我一种全新的视觉景观，让我认识到，美丽和满足近在咫尺，只要细心发现就能唾手可得。

hand within the range of one's own sensibilities.

It made me think, then and later, about other matters to which this incident was related. It helped me realize that there is no sense in my attempting ever to flee from circumstances and conditions which cannot be avoided but which I might bravely meet and frequently mend and often turn to good account. I know that half the battle is won if I can face trouble with courage, disappointment with spirit, and triumph with humility. It has become ever clearer to me that danger is far from disaster, that defeat may be the forerunner of final victory, and that, in the last analysis, all achievement is perilously fragile unless based on enduring principles of moral conduct.

I have learned that trying to find a carefree world somewhere far off involves me in an endless chase in the course of which the opportunity for happiness and the happiness of attainment are all too I often lost in the chase itself. It has become apparent to me that I cannot wipe out the pains of existence by denying them, blaming them largely or completely on others, or running away from them.

The elements of weakness which mark every person cannot absolve me from the burdens and blessings of responsibility for myself and to others. I can magnify but never lessen my problems by ignoring, evading or exercising them. I believe that my perplexities and difficulties can be considerably resolved, if not completely overcome, by my own attitudes and actions. I am convinced that there can be no guarantee of my happiness except that I help evoke and enhance it by the work of my hands and the dictates of my heart and the direction of my striving.

这件事从此也指引着我去思考相关的事情。它让我意识到，对于无法避免的环境与条件，企图逃避没有任何意义，但我可以勇敢地面对它们，并常常进行修补改善。我知道，只要我能勇敢地面对困难、失望而不沮丧，成功而不骄傲，人生之战就取得了一半的胜利。我也更清楚地意识到，危险远非灾难，而失败可能就是最终胜利的先行者。因此，归根结底，所有成就如果不经受道德准则的考验，就会脆弱不堪。

我懂了，当自己无尽地追逐着，试图在遥远之地找到一个无忧无虑的世界时，也常常会在追逐中错过获得幸福与成就的机会。显然，拒绝承认生存的痛苦，将它们多数或全部归咎于他人，或者逃避，都无法将它消除。

每个人都有弱点，但我为自己和他人排忧解难以及祈求祝福的责任并不能因此免除。我可以放大问题，却绝不会为缩小问题而忽视、逃避或求助神灵。我相信，通过自己的态度和行为，我可以很大程度上解决我的疑惑和困难，即使无法克服全部。我相信，要想使幸福有所保障，接受心灵的指引，就必须靠自己的双手，朝着目标努力奋斗，去创造并积累幸福。

Left Behind
遗留在时光背后的思念

◎ Pamela Perry Blaine

They're gone now.

I stood in the driveway and watched my grown children drive off into the distance. I looked down the road until I could no longer see their vehicles.

"They live way too far away from me," I said to myself. "When did they grow up and become parents of small children? Shouldn't that be me?"

I slipped back inside the house and just walked through the rooms for no reason in particular. I was just missing them already and looking for signs of their having been here. There were pillows on the floor where they had been tossed from the couch and a few stuffed animals lying around where the children had been playing.

I smiled at the little fingerprints on my mirror. I didn't wipe them off. I thought back to the time when I tried so hard to keep the fingerprints off the mirrors and doors when my children were small. Now, I wanted the tiny fingerprints to stay so that I could see them there just a little longer.

As I walked around the house, I picked up a few items on the floor and straightened a chair. I decided to sort through the toy box and I found a flying dinosaur, a skeleton, and a Frankenstein that had mysteriously taken up residence

名人语库

To have a child is to decide forever to have your heart go walking around outside your body.

Elizabeth Stone

有了孩子，就永远注定你的心将游离体外。

伊丽莎白·斯通（美国作家）

现在他们走了。

我站在车道上，看着我那已长大的孩子渐渐驶远。我凝视着路的尽头，直到再也看不见他们的身影。

“他们住得离我太远了，”我自言自语道，“他们什么时候长大并为人父母的？我不是才长大，才为人父母吗？”

我回到屋里，只是在各个房间里漫无目的地游荡。他们刚刚离去，我的思念就开始蔓延了，我只好在屋里寻找着他们曾逗留的痕迹。地板上散落着孩子们从沙发上扔下来的枕头，一些布绒玩具动物正躺在孩子们之前玩耍的地方。

我对着镜子上的小指印微笑，没有将它们擦去。回想起当我的孩子还小时，我都尽力不让镜子和房门沾上指印。现在，我希望这些小指印都留在上面，这样我就能看久一点。

当我在房间里游荡时，我捡起地上的一些物品，并把一张椅子拉正。我决定整理一下玩具箱里的玩具。而我发现了一只会飞的恐龙、一个动物骨架，连弗兰肯斯坦这个小怪人也不知怎么就神秘地跑到玩具箱里了。

in my box of toys.

I walked into the kitchen and there on the back of the sink was a bottle brush that had been left behind. "Ah, even Tessa left something behind," I announced. Well, I suppose she had help since she was just four months old.

"I wonder what else has been left behind," I said out loud to no one in particular. My husband heard me and joined the search for things left behind.

It seems like every time our family gets together something is left behind. When I call my children to tell them what they have left behind I am usually told, "Oh, just bring it when you come," "Keep it for me until I come back the next time," or "Hey, I really need that, would you mind mailing it to me?"

"Oh look! Here's Tegan's tooth," I said to my husband as I picked up a ziplock bag with her name engraved on it. Tegan had a loose tooth and had managed to wiggle it out earlier in the day. "Now, she can't put it under her pillow. I wonder if it will work if I put it under my pillow. The Tooth Fairy is going to be so confused!" I laughed.

I walked on around the house finding more things that had been left behind: a toothbrush, a ponytail band, an angel figurine, a pie pan, a frozen teething ring in the freezer, and last but not least the insides of a turkey fryer.

I was really kind of enjoying myself. It gave me something to do, after they left, to take my mind off of missing them.

Then my eyes teared up as I noticed the baby outfit beside the sink where it had been left to dry after spots had been scrubbed out of it. The little outfit, now stain free, reminded me of the trip to the emergency room with Rowan due to a gash on her head that was caused from a flower pot pulled over by her curious little fingers.

"Hmmm, things left behind…" I pondered to myself. It seems there is one

我走进厨房，水槽后面有一个落下的洗瓶刷。“啊，连特莎也落下了一个东西。”我说道。噢，肯定是有人帮她刷瓶子才落下的，因为她只有四个月大呢。

“还落下了些什么东西呢。”我大声地自言自语道。我丈夫听见了我的话，也和我一块搜寻那些落下的物品。

似乎每次我们家庭聚会，他们总会落下一些东西。每次我打电话给我的孩子，告诉他们落下了些什么时，他们通常都会跟我说：“噢，下次你来时给我们带上吧。”或者“帮我留着，下次我回去再拿。”又或者“嗨，我急需要用，能帮我邮寄过来吗？”

“嘿，你看！这是泰根的牙齿。”我捡起一个写着她名字的自封袋，对丈夫说道。泰根先前有一颗牙齿松了，今早她设法把它拽了下来。“现在，她没法把牙放在她的枕头下了。不知道如果把它放在我的枕头下，那传说是否会奏效。牙仙子会很困惑的！”我笑了。

我在房间里四处游走，发现了更多落下的东西：一把牙刷、一根发带、一个天使小雕像、一个烙饼平底锅、一个放在冰箱里冷藏给婴儿长牙时咬的橡皮环，最后还有一个同样重要的火鸡油炸锅内胆。

这还真是让我乐在其中。这让我在他们离开后有事可做，从而暂时摆脱对他们的思念。

然后，当我留意到水槽旁晾着的那件已被洗净的婴儿服时，我的泪水涌了上来。那件干净的小衣服让我想起了我与罗温的急诊室之行。那次，她用好奇的小手指拉倒了一个花瓶，碎片在她头上划开了一道很深的伤口。

“嗯，落下的东西……”我陷入一片沉思之中。似乎有一样东西每次都

thing that is left behind on every occasion. Memories are always left behind, I reasoned, and what a precious thing good memories are to us. I thought how each item left behind reminded me of the person it belonged to and the story surrounding it. The insides of the turkey fryer that was left behind reminded me of the delicious Thanksgiving meal that we all enjoyed. The empty pie pan reminded me of Katie's delicious pies. The angel figurine reminded me of the white elephant gift exchange game that we play every year. Even the bad memory of Rowan's injury reminded me of how frightened I was at the sound of her cry. It is a bad memory that turned into a good one as it reminded us of how precious little Rowan is to us.

Memories happen even if we aren't aware of it. The stressful and difficult moments often become memories that we look back on later with laughter and joy. They are the stories of the future when one day someone will say, "Remember when...?", and everyone laughs.

Then, of course, there are some memories that need to be left behind. The memories of past hurts, unforgiveness, bitterness, and anger should be left behind forever. These are the things that we should never keep until the next time, mail back, or bring with us to our next visit.

Yes, I stood in the driveway and watched my grown children drive off into the distance and I remembered my own parents once doing the same thing. I never knew then that I would one day be the one waving from the driveway and feeling my heart drive off down the road. That's because there is one more thing besides memories left behind... and that is love.

会被落下。记忆，我寻思着，美好的记忆对我们来说是如此珍贵。我想着，每一件落下的物品都使我回想起对物主和相关故事的追忆。那个火鸡油炸锅内胆，使我想起了我们都很享受的那顿美味的感恩节大餐；空空的烙饼平底锅，使我想起了卡蒂的美味馅饼；天使小雕像，使我想起了我们每年都会玩的“白象礼物交换游戏”。甚至关于罗温受伤的那段不好的记忆，也使我想起了听到她的哭喊声时，我有多么害怕。这个糟糕的记忆之所以变得美好，是因为它提醒了我，小罗温对我们来说是多么珍贵。

即便是在我们毫不知情的时刻，记忆也总是在不断发生。当我们回顾往事时，我们会对那些充满压力和困难的时刻报以微笑和喜悦。未来的某天里，有人会问：“还记得……那个时候吗？”这时，大家都会会心大笑起来。

接下来，当然，也有一些需要被放下的记忆。过去的一些伤害、怨恨、痛苦或愤怒的记忆，应该永远放下。我们永不该把这些记忆留存至下次见面的时候，不该用以回敬他人，也不要带到他人面前。

是的，我站在车道上，看着我那已长大的孩子渐渐驶远。我想起了我的父母也曾做过同样的事。我从不知道，有一天，我也会在车道上向远方挥手，感受着自己的心在那条路上驶远。那是因为，除了留下的记忆以外，还有一样东西也留下了……那就是爱。

Make It Come True

梦想照进现实

◎ Dan Clark

In 1957, a ten year old boy in California set a goal. At that time Jim Brown was the greatest running back ever to play pro football and this tall, skinny boy wanted his autograph. In order to accomplish his goal, the young boy had to overcome some obstacles.

He grew up in the ghetto, where he never got enough to eat. Malnutrition took its toll and a disease called rickets forced him to wear steel splints to support his skinny bow out legs. He had no money to buy a ticket to get into the game, so he waited patiently near the locker room until the game ended and Jim Brown left the field. He politely asked Brown for his autograph. As Brown signed, the boy explained “Mr. Brown, I have all your pictures on my wall. I know you hold all the records. You are my idol.”

Brown smiled and began to leave, but the young boy was not finished. He proclaimed, “Mr. Brown, one day I am going to break every record you hold!” Brown was impressed and asked, “what’s your name, son?”

The boy replied, “Orenthal James Simpson. My friends call me O.J.”

O. J Simpson went on to break all but three of the rushing records held by Jim Brown before injuries shortened his football career.

Goal setting is the strongest force for human motivation.

Set a goal and make it come true.

名人语库

Don't believe that winning is really everything. It's more important to stand for something. If you don't stand for something, what do you win?

Lane Kirkland

不要认为取胜就是一切，更重要的是要有信念。倘若你没有信念，那胜利又有什么意义呢？

莱恩·柯克兰（美国工党领袖）

1957 年，加利福尼亚有一个 10 岁小男孩立下了目标。当时，吉姆·布朗是最有名的职业足球运动员，而这个高高瘦瘦的小男孩很想要他的签名。为了能实现愿望，这个年轻的小男孩必须战胜种种阻碍。

他在贫民窟里长大，在那儿始终都吃不饱。营养不良导致他患上“佝偻病”，这使他不得不带上钢夹板以支撑那瘦弱弯曲的腿。他没钱买票去看比赛，所以他就耐心地呆在更衣室里，直到比赛结束、吉姆离场的那一刻。他很礼貌地问吉姆要他的亲笔签名。在吉姆签名时，这个男孩解释道：“布朗先生，我的墙上挂满了你所有的照片。我知道你保持的所有比分记录。你是我的偶像。”

布朗笑了笑，准备离开，但这个年轻的小男孩并没有停下脚步。他向布朗宣称道：“布朗先生，总有一天我要打破你的所有记录！”这给布朗留下了深刻的印象，他问道：“孩子，你叫什么名字？”

男孩回答道：“O.J. 辛普森。朋友们都叫我 O.J.。”

在 O.J. 辛普森因受伤终止自己的足球生涯之前，除了由吉姆·布朗保持的三项带球冲刺记录外，他一举打破了其他全部记录。

设定目标是激励个人动力的最强的力量。

设定目标，然后实现它。

Good Memories—the Gift That Keeps on Giving

美好的记忆——永恒的礼物

◎ Michael Josephson

In a world preoccupied with the quest for material possessions, it's easy to overlook the fact that the most valuable things we own are our best memories. Good memories are the gift that keeps on giving. They make us smile, feel proud, and re-experience the pleasure of past times.

Looked at through the soft lens of sentiment, even the memory of cranky relatives and family traditions that bored or annoyed us at the time can be heart warming links with our past.

But whether your memories of the holiday season conjure up good feelings and happy sounds, smells, and tastes or negative feelings filled with disappointments, resentments, and grudges, I hope you'll resolve this year to consciously create lasting good memories for yourself and those you care about.

Although few of us remember what we gave or got last year or the year before, the tendency is to put too much emphasis on the process of giving and getting gifts.

Don't worry so much about what to buy your family and friends; think more about what you want to give them.

Think beyond the synthetic atmosphere of the mall. Prefabricated

名人语库

The supreme happiness of life is the conviction that we are loved.

V. Hugo

生活中最大的幸福是坚信有人爱我们。

雨果（法国文学家）

在这个世界上，一心只忙于追求物质财富，就很容易忽视这样一个事实：我们所拥有的最珍贵的东西是我们最美好的回忆。美好的记忆是赐予我们的礼物。它让我们面带笑容，心生自豪，并重温过去的愉快时光。

透过那些多愁善感的记忆镜头，甚至某些时刻偏执的亲人、无聊而恼人的家庭传统，这些记忆与我们过去的时光相连，也会变得温暖人心。

但是，不管这些记忆节日是充满愉悦的心境和快乐的声音、味道、气息，还是充斥着失望、愤怒和怨恨，我希望你今年能下意识地去创造持久而美好的回忆，为你自己，也为你所在乎的人。

尽管很少有人记得我们在去年或前年收到了什么，送出了什么，但我们更应该注重给予或获得礼物的美好过程。

不要太担心你要给家人和朋友买些什么；多想想你希望给予他们什么。

decorations and gift certificates are not the stuff of lasting recollections. Think about the feelings you want to create.

The best memories are made out of simple stuff—homemade food, handmade gifts, heartfelt letters, good conversations, games, and heirlooms.

Highlight and celebrate old traditions and consciously create new ones. You'll be glad you did—for a long time.

多想想大型商场氛围以外的东西。订制的装饰品和礼品单据并不属于永久的回忆。多想想你想要创造什么样的感觉。

最好的回忆都是由最简单的东西组成——自制食品，手工礼品，用心的信件，愉快的聊天，游戏以及祖传遗物。

重视并庆祝一些古老的传统日，并有意创造一些新的纪念。你会为你这么做了而感到高兴——久久地因此而快乐着。

The Uncertainty Principle
生活的不确定性

◎ Adam Khan

Two sailors ran into each other in a pub. Over a few beers, one of the men told the other about his last voyage: "After a month at sea," he said, "we discovered our masts had been eaten through by termites! Almost nothing left of them."

"That's terrible," said the second sailor.

"That's what I thought at first too," the first sailor said, "but it turned out to be good luck. As soon as we took the sails down to fix the masts, we were hit by a squall so suddenly and so hard, it would surely have blown us over if our sails were up at the time."

"How lucky!"

"That's exactly what I thought at the time, too. But because our sails were down, we couldn't steer ourselves, and because of the wind, we were blown onto a reef. The hole in the hull was too big to fix. We were stranded."

"That is bad luck indeed."

"That's what I thought, too, when it first happened. But we all made it to the beach alive and had plenty to eat. But now here's the real kicker: while we were on the island whining about our terrible fate, we discovered a buried treasure!"

名人语库

We must accept finite disappointment, but we must never lose infinite hope.

Martin Luther King

我们必须接受失望，因为它是有限的；但千万不可失去希望，因为它是无穷的。

马丁·路德·金（美国民权运动领袖）

两名水手在一间酒吧里偶遇对方。几瓶啤酒下肚后，其中一个人向另一个说起了他的最后一次航行："在海上的一个月后，"他说，"我们发现我们的桅杆都被白蚁啃透了！它们几乎啃得一干二净，什么都没有留下。"

"这真是太可怕了。"另一个水手说。

"我最开始也是这么想的，"第一个水手说，"但它原来却是幸运的事儿呢。正当我们把帆拿下来，准备修复桅杆时，突然遭受到一股强劲的阵风，如果我们的帆当时还挂在上面的话，它肯定会将我们都吹走的。"

"多么幸运啊！"

"我当时也是这么想的。但因为我们的帆都取下来了，我们不能引导自己的方向，而且因为这阵大风，我们都被吹到了礁石上。船体上的洞太大而无法修复。所以我们被困住了。"

"那还是运气不好。"

"那时我也是这么想的。但我们到海滩上的所有人都活着，还有足够的东西吃。而这里才是真正棒的地方：当我们在岛上抱怨命运的可怕时，我们却发现了埋藏的宝藏！"

As this story illustrates, you don't know if an event is "good" or "bad" except maybe in retrospect, and even then you don't really know because life keeps going. The story's not over yet. Just because something hasn't turned out to be an advantage yet doesn't mean it is not ever going to.

Therefore, you can simply assume whatever happens is "good".

I know that sounds awfully airy-fairy, but it's very practical. If you think an event is good, it's easy to maintain a positive attitude. And your attitude affects your health, it affects the way people treat you and how you treat others, and it affects your energy level. And those can help pave the way for things to turn out well. A good attitude is a good thing. And a bad attitude does you no good at all.

So get in the habit of saying "That's good!" Since you don't know for sure whether something will eventually work to your advantage or not, you might as well assume it will. It is counterproductive to assume otherwise. Think about it.

If someone ahead of you in line at a store is slowing everything down, say to yourself, "That's good!" They may have saved you from getting into an accident when you get back in your car. Or maybe, because you slowed down, you might meet a friend you would have missed. You never know.

The truth is, life is uncertain. And even that can work to your advantage.

这个故事说明了，一个事件是“好事”还是“坏事”你并不知道，也许只有在回想起来时才明白；因为生活总会继续下去，所以你根本无从得知它的好坏。这个故事还没有结束。因为有些事情还没有被证明是好事，但这并不意味着它永远都不是好事。

因此，你可以简单地假设，无论发生什么，它都是“好事”。

我知道这听起来像是空谈，但它的确很奏效。如果你认为一件事是好事，你就很容易保持积极的态度。你的态度会影响你的健康，会影响人们对你的方式以及你对待他人的方式，它会影响你的能量高度。那些能帮你铺平道路，让事情变好。一个好态度是件好事。糟糕的态度对你毫无益处。

所以，养成说“那很好！”的习惯。既然你不确定某件事是否最终会对你有利，你不妨假设它会。否则的话，它会适得其反。想一想。

如果商店里排在你前面的人慢下来时，对自己说：“那很好！”他们可能因此在你返回车里时救你脱离一场交通意外。或者，因为你放慢速度，你可能会遇到一个本会错过的朋友。你永远不知道会发生什么。

事实是，生活是不确定的。而且甚至常常充满了好运。

点滴改变，收获精彩

It is better to waste one's youth than to do nothing with it at all.

年轻时做一点儿事，要比什么事也不做好。

Relax, Smile, and Create
放松，微笑，创造

◎ Jessie

Relax

Don't take yourself too seriously.

Happiness is largely a choice.

Feel gratitude for all of the good in your life.

Smile

Once you have enough to pay for life's basics think to yourself: "I've won."

Happiness is contagious: find someone who is happy and stand close to them.

Play, Create

Happiness is attainable.

Slow down and enjoy the scenery. Be spontaneous.

Happiness is perched on your windowsill, invite it in.

Success is not the key to happiness; happiness is the key to success.

Surround yourself with positive, life-affirming people.

名人语库

Fear not that thy life shall come to an end, but rather fear that it shall never have a beginning.

J. H. Newman

不要害怕你的生活将要结束，应该担心你的生活永远不曾真正开始。

纽曼（英国教育家）

放松

不要把自己看得太重。

快乐在很大程度上，是一种选择。

为你生命中的所有美好而心存感激。

微笑

一旦你能满足自己的基本生活需求了，就对自己说：“我赢了。”

快乐是会传染的：找到那些快乐的人，和他们并肩前行。

玩，创造

快乐是可以获得的。

慢下来，去欣赏沿途的风景。要发自内心。

快乐就栖息在你的窗台，邀请它进来吧。

成功不是快乐的必然；而快乐却是成功的关键。

争取让你身边环绕着那些积极而又生活乐观的人。

Make others happy.

Have big dreams.

Enjoy the journey.

Grab every single morsel of happiness which comes your way.

Be on the look out for moments of pleasure and wonder.

带给别人快乐。

拥有大大的梦想。

享受旅途。

抓住沿途中点点滴滴的快乐。

珍惜每个开心和奇迹的瞬间。

A Simple Way to Improve Your Life Everyday
简单一小步，丰富每一天

© Donald Latumahina

I love to have simple ways to improve my life. Everyday is a chance for improving our life, and it's up to us to best use it. What I want is to have good, balanced progress everyday.

To ensure balance, my favorite way is using the four facets of prosperity: material, spiritual, physical, and social. By achieving material prosperity, spiritual prosperity, physical prosperity, and social prosperity, I believe I can have complete and balanced prosperity in my life.

You may add other facets of prosperity if they work for you, but in my opinion these four facets are easy to remember and already cover practically everything.

To put this concept into practice, what I do is ensuring that I do something to improve each facet everyday. Here is how I do it:

1. Decide on something to do daily in each facet

To keep things simple, choose only one or two tasks to do daily in each facet. More than that, it could be difficult to keep up with them. Of course, you may want to do more than just one or two tasks to improve a facet, but choose

名人语库

We have no more right to consume happiness without producing it than to consume wealth without producing it.

George Bernard Shaw

正像我们无权只享受财富而不创造财富一样，我们也无权只享受幸福而不创造幸福。

萧伯纳（爱尔兰剧作家）

我喜欢用简单的方法提高自己的生活水平。对我们的生命来说，每一天都是一个新的机遇，而它则取决于我们如何最有效地利用它。我所希望的，是每天都有良好、平稳的提高。

我最倾向于通过物质生活、精神境界、身体素质、社交活动四个方面的互补来保持生活的平衡。如果可以达到物质富足、精神愉悦、身体健康以及社交活跃，那么我相信，我一定会拥有和谐美妙而精彩纷呈的生活。

当然啦，你还可以添加一些你认为有用的东西。不过，在我看来，以上四个方面易于记忆，而且基本已经涵盖了一切。

为了将这个观念付诸实践，我每天都会努力来完善这四方面。下面是我个人的做法：

1. 决定每天在每方面所要做的事

把事情简单化，每天每个方面只选择一两个任务。当然，坚持下来还是有一定难度的。为了提高某方面，你可能每天不止要做一两个任务，不过记住，选择最重要的去做。就我的情况而言，每天我只针对一个方面做

only the most important ones to be made daily. In my case, I have just one task for each facet.

One thing to remember is each of the tasks should be measurable so that you know for sure whether or not you have done it. Here is an example:

* Material: do project for at least 2 hours

* Spiritual: meditate for 30 minutes

* Physical: exercise for 20 minutes

* Social: ping at least one friend

2. Record your performance

After setting the daily tasks for each facet, all you need to do is ensuring that you do them. Recording your performance can greatly help you here. You may use a notebook, a spreadsheet, or any other medium you want. Write down there whether or not you have done a task in a particular day.

3. Adjust accordingly

If you think that you can more effectively improve yourself doing something else, don't hesitate to change the tasks. For example, maybe you think that reading spiritual text will give you better result than meditation for spiritual prosperity. In that case, you can change your daily task from meditation to reading spiritual text. On the other hand, if you think that they are both necessary, you can decide to do both (though you shouldn't forget to keep things simple).

Another possibility is increasing the intensity of the tasks to bring you to the next level. For instance, instead of exercising for 20 minutes a day, you could make it 30 minutes a day.

By using this system, you can be sure that you do something everyday to

一项任务。

还有一点要记住，你所做的每项活动都应当有可衡量的标准，这样你才能确定自己是否已经完成了。下面举个例子：

* 物质方面：至少工作 2 小时

* 精神方面：自我反省 30 分钟

* 身体方面：运动 20 分钟

* 社交方面：至少和一个朋友闲聊

2. 记录你的进度

在制定每天的各方面任务后，你要做的就是确保自己有所行动。记录每日进度是个很有效的办法。你可以用一个笔记本、电子表格或任何你想用的工具，记录你一天之内是否已经完成任务。

3. 适时调整

如果你能通过其他途径更有效地提升自己，那么不要犹豫，果断调整任务吧。比如，也许你认为品读心灵美文比自我反省能更好地提升思想境界，那么你可以把每日反省调整成阅读有关精神方面的文章。另外，如果你觉得这两项都有必要，你可以两个都选（但记住不要让事情复杂化）。

另一种可能就是增加任务的强度，让自己提升到一个更高的水平上。例如，你可以从每天锻炼 20 分钟提升到每天锻炼 30 分钟。

通过实践这套体系，你可以确保每天都在做些提升自己各个方面的事

improve yourself in all facets. It's as if you make balanced progress on autopilot. I've used it for some time and—though I miss my daily tasks here and there—I'm glad to see how it helps me have balanced progress to complete prosperity.

What do you think? Do you have other tips for daily improvement?

情。稳步提升自我似乎变成了一件驾轻就熟之事。我曾经这样做过一段时间——尽管我时常忘这忘那——但值得高兴的是，在稳步提升自己的生活水平方面，它确实对我有所帮助。

你有什么看法呢？对于改善自己的日常生活，你有其他建议吗？

Life as Chopsticks
人生如筷

◎ Jessica

Chopsticks. Right now, millions of people are digging into their food with two sticks that have stood the test of time as a utensil for humans, even when countless thousands of other tools, gadgets and products haven't. But what's so special about them?

What can we learn from mere chopsticks?

Personally, I have used them all my life, but it was only recently I realized the depth of influence they had in many people's way of life. They teach us the importance of:

Simplicity. They can come in all kinds of colors and sizes but essentially they are just two long sticks. There's hardly anything more simple than two bits of wood being pushed together. With new technology being released everyday and adverts bombarding us with the need to be able to do more with less, multi-tasking and multiple-use devices, it is sort of refreshing to still have something which has just one use—simply to eat. Chopsticks are a living example that simplicity simply works, and we don't need to keep developing, improving and fixing things all the time.

Versatility. Chopsticks can be used for picking up all kinds of food; meat, vegetable, rice, even the bones from fish, because by nature, their simplicity means that they are adaptable. Instead of aiming for a niche in an attempt to find

名人语库

Habit is habit, and not to be flung out of the window by any man, but coaxed downstairs a step a time.

Mark Twain

习惯就是习惯，谁也不能将其扔出窗外，只能一步一步地引它下楼。

马克·吐温（美国小说家）

筷子。现如今，当无数的工具、器具和产品都已被时间淘汰时，只有筷子经受住了时间的考验，成千上万的人用它来夹取食物。然而，它究竟有什么特别之处?

从这简单的筷子中，我们可以学到什么?

就我个人而言，我一生都在使用筷子，但直到最近，我才意识到它深深地影响了许多人的生活方式。它教会了我们许多重要的事：

简单。虽然筷子颜色各异，长短不同，但实质上它们就是两根长棍。没有什么比两根靠在一起就能使用的木棍更简单的东西了。在科技日新月异的今天，铺天盖地的广告告诉我们应该使用那些事半功倍的多功能设备，筷子却仍旧保持着单一的用途——只是用来吃饭，这真是让人觉得不同寻常啊。筷子这个活生生的例子说明：简简单单的东西照样能派上用场，我们并不需要总是不断地改善、发展、革新。

多样化。筷子可以用来夹取各种各样的食物，如肉类、蔬菜、米饭，甚至是鱼骨头，因为它们简单的本质就意味着它们的适应性够强。它们能满足各种广泛的要求，而不是只瞄准于弥补某些“市场空白”，或者填充那

a “gap in the market”, or to fill a hole that probably doesn’t need filling, they cater to a wide range purposes. Imagine being like chopsticks in this way, able to appeal to many people because you are useful, without worrying about being “more innovative” or “better” in anyway. They just do what they are made to do; they just are.

Aim. If you’ve ever tried using them, you know that you can’t get what you want by just haphazardly stabbing at the plate. To be able to get what you want, you have to aim for it. There’s no way you can pick up everything in one go. Know what you want, and just do it. Sometimes, a little bit of focus makes the difference between failure and success.

Practice. Using chopsticks doesn’t come naturally. You have to learn to use them and practice it. But how will you learn? Should you just read about it? Most would agree that there’s no better way to practice than to look at the delicious food in front of you and tell yourself that you can’t have any until you can use the chopsticks to get it. In real life, you can read in books as much as you like about all the things you want to do, but it will just amount to dreams and theory if you don’t try actually doing it. Don’t just watch others eating, put yourself out there and give the chopsticks a go.

Slowing Down. A common health tip is to try to eat with chopsticks when you can. Why? Because it slows you down and allows your stomach to tell your brain you’re full before you overeat. Eating with chopsticks is a slower process, but that is not necessarily a bad thing. Sometimes we need to slow down and take things one step at a time, break it down at each stage so that we have time to think, to realize that we’re actually full and that we don’t have to keep charging full speed through life.

Sometimes it’s nice to enjoy each morsel of life as it comes.

些可能没必要填充的空洞。想象一下筷子的哲学：有自己的用途且无需担心被“革新”或被“改善”，所以深受人们喜爱。筷子只是做了它应该做的，筷子就是筷子。

目标。如果你曾试过用筷子吃饭，你就知道在餐盘上随意乱戳是夹不到你想要的东西的。你必须瞄准目标。你不可能一次性夹到所有东西。认清你要什么，然后去做。有时，成功与失败的区别就在于那一点点的准确性。

不断实践。没人生来就会使用筷子。你必须学着使用它们并不断练习。然而，你该怎样学呢？仅仅只是阅读说明书吗？绝大多数人都认可，最好的练习方法是盯着你面前的美食，然后告诉自己不用筷子夹到它就没法吃。在我们的现实生活中，你可以从书中阅读到任何你想要做的事情，但是如果你不试着将其付诸实践，它也就仅仅只是梦想和理论。不要只是看着别人吃，自己也要去拿双筷子，自己去试试。

放慢节奏。一个众所周知的健康秘诀就是尽可能使用筷子吃饭。为什么？因为它会让你放慢节奏，在你吃撑之前，你的胃会告诉你的大脑你已经吃饱了。用筷子吃饭是个缓慢的过程，但这未必是一件坏事。有时候，我们需要放慢脚步，凡事要一步一步，在每个阶段停顿一下，这样我们就有时间去思考，意识到我们其实已经饱了，我们不应该总是保持高速度的生活。

有时候，享受生活的一点一滴是很美好的事。

Yoga for Lowering Stress
开心玩瑜伽，减压好方法

◎ Mary L. Gavin

Yoga and You

When you hear the word "yoga", do you think of a person with his legs twisted up like a pretzel? If so, it may seem like yoga is very complicated or just for adults. Not true! Kids and teens can do yoga for the same reasons grown-ups do: because it feels good to stretch out your body, slow down your breathing, and relax your mind. Yoga can help you feel calmer when life is busy and stressful.

What You Need

Any time you start a new exercise routine it's a good idea to check with a parent. A yoga class can be a great way to get started because the instructor can teach you how to get into the poses. Find a large enough space with few distractions. No TV or people, if possible. Wear comfortable workout clothes and no shoes or socks. A yoga mat can be helpful because it cushions a bit and keeps your feet from slipping. Yoga should not hurt, so go slow and ease into position. Go only as far as you comfortably can.

Why Yoga for Stress?

When you get stressed or nervous, many things can help you feel better. Talking with someone—a parent or friend—is a great idea because they can help

名人语库

People who can not find time for recreation are obliged sooner or later to find time for illness.

John Wanamaker

腾不出时间娱乐的人，早晚会被迫腾出时间生病。

霍梅克.J.（美国商人）

你与瑜伽

当你听到“瑜伽”这个词时，你是否会想到一个人将自己的大腿扭曲成卷饼那样？如果是这样，瑜伽看起来就似乎很复杂，像专门给成人练习的。但事实并非如此！儿童和青少年也可以因为同样的理由练习瑜伽：伸展身体、放慢呼吸、放松思想的感觉很棒。当你感到生活忙碌、压力重重时，瑜伽可以帮助你平静下来。

你需要

无论任何时候，当你开始一项新的锻炼安排时，和家长谈谈总是好的。上瑜伽课程是个不错的开始，因为教练会教你怎样做动作。找一个足够大且很少让你分心的地方。最好不要有电视或其他人。穿上舒适的运动服，不要穿鞋袜。瑜伽垫很有用，因为它有一定的缓冲作用，而且会防止出现脚滑。瑜伽不应该让你感到疼痛，所以你要慢慢地、舒服地摆正姿势。尽量做，舒服就行。

为什么选择瑜伽减压？

当你感到压力或紧张时，很多事都可以让你放松下来。同别人聊聊

you figure out what's wrong and start coming up with solutions. In addition, you can ease stress through exercise. You probably know exercise is good for your health, but it's also a proven way to put you in a better mood. So it makes sense that yoga is a favorite activity among people who want to feel stronger and more relaxed. Yoga includes a lot of stretching, but that's not all—yoga also focuses on breathing and meditation, which means thinking calm thoughts. Practicing yoga is a chance to learn stretching/breathing/thinking skills that you can use to calm yourself down the next time you feel worried. In other words, yoga can help your body stay loose and relaxed when things heat up!

Think Good Thoughts

Meditation is the first part of a stress-relieving yoga routine. Meditation means being calm, quiet, and focused. Some people call this "feeling centered" . When you're feeling centered, you can do your best in stressful situations such as taking a test or working through a disagreement with a friend. Try these meditation exercises: Take a yoga vacation: Find a quiet, private place, like your bedroom. Sit in a comfortable position and close your eyes. Imagine a place where you feel safe and relaxed. Is it your best friend's backyard? Your grandma's house? Camping in the woods? Imagine yourself in this place for three to five minutes. You'll feel much calmer after your "yoga vacation". Positive pictures: When you're feeling stressed about a big test or game, it can help to imagine it going really well. Sit in a comfortable position and close your eyes. Picture yourself feeling prepared for your test or kicking the winning goal in soccer. Of course, positive pictures can't take the place of actual preparation, but they can help you feel more confident.

天——父母或朋友——这方法就很不错，因为他们可以帮你发现问题所在，找出解决方案。此外，你还可以通过体育锻炼减轻压力。你也许知道运动对身体有好处，但它也是一个可以令人心情愉悦的行之有效的办法。所以，对于那些希望变得更强壮、渴望放松下来的人来说，瑜伽就是最受欢迎的运动了。瑜伽包括大量的伸展动作，但它远不止如此——瑜伽还注重呼吸和冥想，也就是平心静气地思考。练习瑜伽让你有机会学习伸展、呼吸以及思考的技巧，下次当你感到忧虑的时候，便可以通过这些让自己冷静下来。换句话说，在事情一团糟的时候，瑜伽可以帮助你舒展和放松身体。

积极的想法

冥想是减压瑜伽训练的第一部分。冥想就是保持平静、安静和专注。有些人称之为“感受中心”。当你感受到自己的中心，在紧张的情况下——比如考试或处理与朋友的分歧等——就能发挥最好状态。试试以下的冥想练习：进行一次瑜伽旅行，找一个安静、私人的地方，比如你的卧室。以舒服的姿势坐下来，闭上双眼。想象一个让你感到安全和放松的地方——挚友的后院？奶奶的房子？还是森林里的露营？用三到五分钟想象你身处这个地方。完成“瑜伽旅行”之后，你会感觉平静多了。积极的画面：当你因为一场大考或比赛而倍感压力时，想象它们进展得十分顺利。舒服地坐下，闭上眼睛。想象那些画面：你已经做好了应考准备，或者有信心在足球赛中踢入致胜一球。当然，想象积极画面不能代替真正的准备工作，但它们能让你更有信心。

Breathe Deep

On one hand, you already know how to breathe. You're doing it right now! But learning how to breathe in yoga practice can help you notice how your breathing changes when you're anxious or upset. Often, when you start to feel nervous or uncomfortable, your breathing may get faster and you might not breathe as deeply. Once you tune in to your breath, you can try belly breathing.

Get Up and Move

There are many different yoga poses. Some can help you stretch the neck, shoulders and back, which are most likely to get tense when you are nervous or stressed. Try these two yoga poses when you want to de-stress yourself: Surprise/Sourpuss: Open your mouth wide and bug out your eyes, then close your eyes very tightly and pucker your lips. Alternate back and forth between "surprise" and "sourpuss". Do this while you're studying to help loosen up your face and jaw, which can get really tense while you're studying. If you have a study partner, make a game of it! Who can make the silliest face? Shoulder gymnastics: Do a few gentle shoulder and neck rolls right before a test to keep your shoulders nice and loose. You can even do them during a test if you need a refreshing break.

Have Fun with Yoga

Yoga can help you in serious ways, but it also can be a lot of fun. You can smile during yoga, and even laugh, which is a great stress reliever too. Yoga can be done alone or with friends. And you can do it at home, at a yoga studio, or in the park. We'll end with a special Sanskrit greeting—"namaste". It's traditionally said at the end of a yoga practice and it means the light inside of me bows to the light inside of you. Namaste.

深呼吸

一方面，你已经知道如何呼吸，因为你此刻就在呼吸！但是，学习如何在瑜伽练习中呼吸，能助你在焦虑不安时发觉呼吸的变化。通常，当你开始感觉紧张不安时，你的呼吸会变得急促，而且呼吸的深度不够。一旦了解自己的呼吸变化，你可以尝试腹部式呼吸。

动起来

瑜伽有许多不同的姿势。有些可以让你伸展颈部、肩膀和背部，这些部位在你紧张或感到压力时通常会绷得很紧。当你想放松自己时，试试以下两个瑜伽姿势：惊喜 / 怒容：张大嘴巴，瞪大双眼，然后紧紧地闭上眼睛，噘起嘴唇。来回交替做“惊讶”和“怒容”这两个动作。学习时，你的脸部和下巴会绷紧，这套动作能帮你放松这两个部位。如果你跟同伴一起学习，还可以当游戏来玩！谁的鬼脸更像呢？肩操：考试前适当摆动肩膀和颈部，这能让你的肩部放松下来。如果想休息一下让自己清醒清醒，你甚至可以在考试中途做这个动作。

开心自在玩瑜伽

瑜伽既可以严肃对待，也可以趣味横生。练习瑜伽时你可以面带笑容，甚至放声大笑，这也是个不错的减压方式。你可以独自练习瑜伽，也可以结伴练习。瑜伽可以在家、瑜伽室或公园里进行。我们将以一句特别的梵文问候语结束——“双手合十”。通常，在瑜伽练习结束时都会说这句话，意思是，我体内的光芒向你体内的光芒鞠躬。双手合十。

Simple Tricks to Boost Your Confidence
着装和微笑带来的改变

◎ Judi James

Take all those clothes that are too small for you to the charity shop. Gazing at wannabe smaller sizes every time you open your wardrobe door is like punching yourself in the eye on a daily basis.

Stop keeping clothes for "best"—wear them regularly.

Smile. Whether you feel like smiling or not, it makes you feel and look better, and other people respond better to you as well.

Stop comparing your life with other people, especially celebrities. Most of them are worried about slipping down the charts or not getting offered the best roles. Their self-obsession means that they are rarely capable of holding down a happy and loving relationship.

Write a proper diary, on paper with a pen. Imagine it's being written for the future you and make it a good account of your life, filled with humor and positive insights. Make your tone brave and optimistic. Adopting this writing style will enable you to change your perspective of what's happening to you.

Compliment yourself. Out loud. In the mirror.

名人语库

Everything can be taken from a man but one thing; the freedom to choose his attitude in any given set of circumstances.

Leonhard Frand

我可以拿走人的任何东西，但有一样东西不行，这就是在特定环境下选择自己的生活态度的自由。

弗兰德（德国小说家）

把那些太小的衣服都捐给慈善店！每天打开衣橱看着那些小得根本穿不进的衣服，就等于是自己戳自己的眼睛啦。

别总把好衣服留在重要场合穿，时不时拿出来穿一穿。

一定要微笑。不管你是否想要笑对一切，这样不仅让自己看上去形象更好，别人也会对你更和善。

别再拿你的生活和别人攀比，尤其不要和名人比。他们大多数人天天担心自己人气下滑，或者担心自己得不到演主角的机会。这种自恋意味着他们根本无法维持一段幸福温馨的感情。

记日记，要用笔写在纸上。想象是写给未来的你看的，为你的人生留下美好的记录，所以语言要幽默积极，口气要勇敢乐观。这种记录风格也会让你从不同的视角来审视当下。

对着镜子大声赞美自己。

My Motivation
我的动力

◎ Erin E.

I used to feel like my life was stressful and hard until a life-changing event happened to my mom's best friend, Anna. She was put in a life-or-death situation and remained strong. Her strength made me want to be like that in my daily life.

One night Anna was coming out of her office building when a man attacked her. He beat her with a rock, took her car keys, and threw her in her car. She told me that she was praying for God to help her the whole time. She knew she would not give up easily, but she also knew they were driving toward the river. The man didn't stop until he absolutely had to. With God's strength, she jumped out of the car and got help.

Anna is not only my mom's friend but also like another mother to me and my sister and brother. When we heard about the attack, we were devastated but so relieved she was alive. My mom became more protective of me, always wanting to know where I was going. I'd never worried about someone attacking or kidnapping me, but now I am more aware of my surroundings and realize that not everyone is as nice as I might think.

Anna stayed strong and optimistic during one of the worst possible situations. Many would have given up, but she didn't. I have so much respect for

名人语库

Courage is the ladder on which all the other virtues mount.

Clare Boothe Luce

勇气是一架梯子，其他美德全靠它爬上去。

卢斯 .C.B.（美国剧作家）

我以前觉得我的生活充满了压力和困难，直到我妈妈最好的朋友——安娜身上发生了一件改变人生的事——在一个生死攸关的境况下，她还仍然保持着坚强。她的力量让我想在日常生活中也变得一样坚强。

一天晚上，安娜走出办公大楼，一个男人袭击了她。他用一块石头打她，抢走了她的车钥匙，并把她扔在她的车上。她告诉我说，她从头到尾一直在祈祷着上帝能给予帮助。她知道她不会轻易放弃，但她也知道他们正在朝河边驶去。这个男人不到必须停车时是不会停下来的。在上帝的力量下，她从车里跳了出来，得到了帮助。

安娜不仅是我妈妈的朋友，对我和我的弟弟妹妹们来说，也像是我们的另一个妈妈。当我们听说了她遭受的攻击时，简直惊呆了，但是她还活着，我们也就放下心来。我妈妈变得更加保护我，时时刻刻都要知道我去了哪里。我从未担心过有人攻击或绑架我，但是现在我更清楚我身边的处境，而且我也意识到，不是每个人都像我想象的那样好。

安娜在最恶劣的情况下，始终保持着坚强、乐观的态度。许多人可能会放弃，但是她没有。我对她是如此尊重，而且希望我能更像她。我从来

her and wish I could be more like her. I have never been through anything like that, but seeing how she responded gave me a desire to be strong and optimistic in my life.

Now, when I think of stress and difficulties, it is not about little everyday problems. Anna truly inspired me not to worry about the small things. She may not know it, but she made me want to be a better person. That is what matters to me: motivation to become a stronger, better individual.

没有经历过像那样的事情，但看到她的经历所给予我的期愿就是，让我在生活中变得坚强、乐观。

现在，每当我想起压力和困难时，它不是关于日常生活的小问题。安娜真正鼓舞我的是不要担心小事情。她可能不知道，是她让我想成为更好的人。这是我所在乎的：拥有动力，成为一个更强大、更完善的人。

An ncounter

一次难忘的邂逅

◎ Megan C.

As the hot tears rolled down her cheeks, I knew I had asked the wrong question. The words reverberated in my mind: widowed or divorced? I looked into the lady's eyes, now dampened with the miserable tears my words had caused.

"Well, you could call me widowed," she replied. "My husband died five months ago today."

Her face, a haunted mask as she looked away, searched the racks as if he might appear. Tears again welled in her eyes, when she didn't find him, and she was unable to blink them back.

"I am so sorry," I mumbled. "I needed it to fill out your credit application." I wished I had allowed her to check the box herself. I knew well enough that words spoken aloud hold more pain than those unspoken.

"Don't worry about it, honey," she soothed. "If I never thought about it, I would not remember the love and the memories we shared. Even after 50 years of marriage, each passing moment would bring a deeper meaning to the word love. Now, trust me, I know how foolish that sounds. We had our share of challenging times, but in the end none of that mattered."

名人语库

The miracle is this—the more we share, the more we have.

Leonard Nimoy

神奇的是我们分享得越多，我们拥有的也越多。

伦纳德·尼莫伊（美国诗人、音乐家）

当热泪顺着她的脸颊流下来时，我知道我问错了问题。这个词在我心中回响：丧偶还是离婚？我看着那位女士的眼睛，现在我的话引起了她悲痛的泪水。

“好吧，你可以说我寡居，”她回答说，“今天是我丈夫去世后的整整五个月。”

她的脸现出愁容，像寻找鬼魂一般向四处搜寻，仿佛他可能会出现。当她没有找到他时，眼泪在她的眼中再一次涌出，她眨着眼睛，无法把眼泪憋回去。

“很抱歉，”我咕哝着，“我需要信息来填写你的信贷申请表。”我真希望我能让她自己检查表格。我知道得很清楚，大声说出来比沉默不语让人更加痛楚。

“别担心，亲爱的，”她安慰我道，“如果我从没想过这些，我就不会记得我们曾共有的爱和回忆。即使在我们的 50 年婚姻之后，每一时刻还是会赋予爱这个词更深层的含义。现在，相信我——我知道这听起来多么愚蠢——我们曾共同承担艰难困苦，但最终都挺过来了。”

Unsure of what to say, I laughed nervously, not yet aware of the impact those words would have on me. I picked up the phone to relay her information; words hung in the air. My mind was not focused on the current task, and I was unsuccessful in my first few attempts. After finally completing the credit application, I turned to find myself riveted to the lady's face again.

Her eyes began to sparkle as she proceeded in a heart-to-heart. I couldn't believe someone could open up to a perfect stranger, but it was not my place to criticize. I enjoyed listening to her just as much as she appreciated having somebody to talk to.

"Have you ever been married?" she asked.

I couldn't help but laugh. I hadn't even thought about getting married. Besides, I looked nothing like a married woman—my braces stuck out from my mouth, and my frizzy hair was thrown back into a messy bun.

"Ah, no." I replied. "I'm only 16."

"Sixteen?" she murmured, eyes alight with the mystery of shrouded memories. "That's a great age, an age of lessons. There's so much worth learning."

She then spoke in a hushed whisper, sharing the one lesson that I will carry with me the rest of my life. "Never, ever take anyone for granted. If you are in love with someone, let it be known as often as you feel it. Otherwise, life may pass you by. Don't spend your life angry. The ridiculous arguments you think are important won't even be remembered in a short time."

Then, she hugged me and thanked me for letting her talk. As she turned to walk away, I could see that tears still hung in her eyes, but the smile that lit her face was amazing. After she left, I stood there replaying the conversation in my mind and letting her words sink in. Never, ever take anyone for granted. If you

不知道该说什么，我紧张地笑了笑，没有意识到这些话会对我产生影响。我拿起电话来汇报她的信息；言语就这样回荡在空中。我的头脑无法专注于当前的任务，这是我第一次尝试好几次专注却都失败了。在最后完成信贷申请程序后，我发现自己再一次不自觉关注起那位女士的脸。

在她继续和我谈心时，她的眼睛开始闪耀着光亮。我不敢相信有人会对一个完全陌生的人打开心扉。但这不是我该指责的地方。我很喜欢听她说话，正如她十分感激有人可以聆听她的言语一样。

“你结婚了吗？”她问。

我忍不住笑了。我还没想过结婚。此外，我一点都不像已婚女人——我的牙套从我嘴里露出来，我卷曲的头发盘成一个凌乱的髻。

“啊，没有。”我回答说，“我还只有 16 岁。”

“16 岁吗？”她喃喃地说，眼神仿佛笼罩在记忆的神秘面纱下，“这个年岁棒极了，一个适合学习的最佳年龄。有这么多的事值得学习呢。”

然后，她安静地低语着，与我分享了一个我余生都会时刻谨记的教导。“永远不要把任何人的爱视为理所当然。如果你爱上某人，让他像你一样常常感受到爱。否则，你可能就会错过属于你的人生。不要让自己活在懊恼之中。有些你认为很重要的荒谬言论，甚至并不会在短时间内被人记住。”

然后，她拥抱了我，并感谢我让她说了这么多。当她转身走开时，我看到眼泪仍挂在她的眼角，但她脸上的微笑却让她的脸显得如此迷人。她离开后，我站在那里回想着我们的谈话，在脑海里重复着她的言语。永远不要把任何人的爱视为理所当然。如果你爱上某人，让他像你一样常常感

are in love with someone, let it be known as often as you feel it.

I have never seen that woman again, but her words of inspiration still live in me. At that time, the words were only little bits of advice. Now, however, they are the words which I try to live by, words that will always remind me of my special friend.

受到爱。

我从未再见过那个女人，但她的话语仍然伴随着我。当时，这些话仅仅只是一个微不足道的小建议。然而现在，我却靠着这些话而生活着，它总是让我记起我特别的朋友。

Make a Plan and Make It Work

让计划动起来

◎ Douglas Lurton

When you determine what you want you have made the most important decision of your life. To attain what you want you must have a plan. Actually, planning is a simple process, but it is amazing how many persons survive without planning. They survive but they do not attain the full richness that life has to offer.

Most of the failures in life are due to lack of planning or to faulty planning. Whatever you may want to accomplish, whether it be the building of a boat, a rise in pay, or the building of a successful career, your chances of success are immeasurably increased by observing these underlying principles of planning.

1. Determine your objective and visualize it. Picture what you want and the kind of person you want to be. Visualize yourself in the boss's private office; in that full professorship; as the president of the bank or factory; as the surgeon performing the miracle of saving life.

2. Get the facts. Get all the facts about what will be required to attain the objective you have determined upon and visualized.

3. Analyze, evaluate, group those facts. Put them in logical order of importance of accomplishment. Put them in a flexible order of accomplishment,

名人语库

If you wish to succeed, you should use persistence as your good friend, experience as your reference, prudence as your brother and hope as your sentry.

Thomas Edison

如果你希望成功，当以恒心为良友，以经验为参谋，以谨慎为兄弟，以希望为哨兵。

爱迪生（美国发明家）

当你明确自己想要什么时，你已经做出了人生中最重大的决定。为了实现这个目标，你必须有一个计划。事实上，制定计划是个简单的过程，然而令人吃惊的是，竟然有很多人在毫无计划地活着。他们活着，却没有充分领悟生活所能给予的充实和丰盛。

人生中大多数的失败都源于缺乏计划或计划不当。无论你想实现什么——是造一条小船，是涨工资，还是开创一项成功的事业——只要你能遵循计划背后的种种规则，成功的机会就会大大增加。

1. 确定你的目标，并想象目标实现时的情景。确定你想要什么，以及你想要成为什么样的人。想象自己坐在老板的办公室里；想象自己成为大学教授；想象自己成为银行家或工厂老板；想象自己成为挽救生命奇迹的医生。

2. 搜集基本信息。弄清楚实现自己的目标有哪些要求。

3. 分析和评估这些信息，并将其分类。将这些要求按照实现的重要程度进行逻辑排序，按照实现的先后灵活排序；同时，还要确保这个顺序符

be sure they are attainable in order, make certain they are practical.

4. Adopt a timetable for the accomplishment of your objective and cleave to that timetable.

5. Have faith, clear, abiding faith, in the ultimate attainment of your objective and the minor objectives that contribute to the whole program of accomplishment. Don't let anyone—friend, relative, or foe—divert you for long from the way in which you know you must go.

6. Take action today to put your plan into effect. A plan without action is a futile dream. Let go of the ball. Don't be content to be continually winding up; you have to let go of the ball to make a strike.

7. Persistently take steps to further your plans. Don't let obstacles get you down. Washouts on the way may delay you, but you can go around or over if you refuse to surrender.

8. Concentrate on one good step at a time and don't walk in more than one direction.

9. Regularly check up on yourself and others assisting you on the way. Adjust your plans as required by circumstances you can't control. Study and follow your timetable.

10. Put your plan and timetable on paper.

Men without plans are at the mercy of the vagrant winds of fortune. Men with plans and determination to follow them have control of their destiny. The choicest prizes that life has to offer go to those who make plans. The leftovers go to the aimless.

合实际。

4. 为实现目标制定时间表，并恪守这个时间表。

5. 在实现终极目标和组成它的小目标的过程中心存信念，此信念务必清晰而持久。不要让任何人——朋友、亲戚或敌人——分散你的注意力，令你心猿意马。

6. 今天就采取行动，将你的计划付诸实践。没有行动的计划无异于白日梦。放手去干吧，不要满足于来回兜圈子，放手一搏才能给予最有力的一击。

7. 坚持不懈，步步为营，让计划越走越长远。不要让任何障碍阻挡你前进的步伐。也许你会在路上遭遇挫折，但如果不想投降，就必须绕过它或跨越它。

8. 每次只专注于一个方面，不要同时进行几项工作。

9. 定期对自己和一路上帮助你的人进行反思。根据实际情况调整计划。研究并遵循你的时间表。

10. 将你的计划和时间表写在纸上。

没有计划的人总是受制于无常的命运，有计划、有决心的人才能掌握自己的人生。生命中最好的奖品总是奖励给那些制定计划并实施计划的人，剩下的人只是漫无目的地游荡。

How to Love Yourself, Even if No One Else Does
怎样爱自己，即使没人爱

◎ Torley

First, the second part of that title isn't true. You either forgot who loves you, or need to find more people who do.

But there may be times where you feel alone and depressed—just about everyone has spells like that, or is strong enough to admit it. It's not easy to talk about, but loneliness, feeling unwanted, and even self-hate from time to time is extremely common. If your hermiting drags on for weeks, you'll want the help of healthcare experts, but if it's not so severe and happens on occasion, here's some vibrant and practical suggestions for you:

Gather a "praise pile"

Ideally, you'll want to do this before you're in a downer—it serves as a life preserver when you're in the "eye of the storm".

Compile the love you've felt: a handwritten note from your Mom, a photo of you and your best buds at the lake together, and awards you've won. They don't have to be recent—recognition spans your whole life. And they don't have to be physical, either; I've used the Firefox ScrapBook add-on to do what its offline analogue does: clip and save kind words from others.

名人语库

A man is not old as long as he is seeking something. A man is not old until regrets take the place of dreams.

J. Barrymore

只要一个人还有追求，他就没有老。直到后悔取代了梦想，一个人才算老。

巴里摩尔（美国演员）

首先，标题的第二部分是不对的。你不会忘记那些爱你的人，也不需要找更多爱你的人。

但有些时候你可能会感觉孤独和沮丧——几乎每个人都这样说过，或者这么承认过。说这些并不容易，但经常孤独、感觉不被需要，甚至自厌都是很常见的。如果你的孤独症状拖上了好几周，你可能需要健康护理专家的帮助了，但如果没有那么严重，只是偶尔才发生，这里有一些实用的好建议：

收集“赞美集册”

理想情况下，你会想在服用镇定剂之前做这些——在你处于“暴风之眼”时，它会充当救生工具。

收集你所感觉到的关爱：妈妈手写的函件，你和最好的朋友在湖边的合影，你所赢得的所有奖励。这些不必是最近发生的，你整个一生中的都行。此外，也没必要是物质上的。我通常使用火狐软件的剪贴薄来添加离线消息；点击并保存别人给我的友好话语。

So when I feel like I'm not being cared about, I take a quick look at the "praise pile", and put what's happening in perspective: others have cared about me before, and they will again. And perhaps most importantly, by realizing this, I care about myself. This is a process and never happens immediately. One can't instantly "snap out of it". It "takes time", as the trite-but-true saying goes. But oh, how true it is.

Give up on something worth dropping

Burdens are bedfellows with loneliness. Some people who'd like to have more of a social life are crushed by the rat race, or their own compounded fears which hold them back. By dropping what I often call "slop" (waste unnecessary to your enjoyment of life), it frees you to take on more meaningful things (keep reading!). Less worry means more freedom to self-explore and pursue interests.

Why does this sound so obvious? Because it is. But it may only be during a time of emotional inner turbulence that you can summon the strength to unchain yourself.

Don't overthink—that makes it worse. As any great performer knows, and as controversial as "muscle memory" may be, repeated practice leads to what's dubbed "second nature", or a threshold surpassed in which analyzing evolves to intuition based on past experiences.

When you find yourself especially stressed or anxious, those are otherwise-unpleasant moments you can use to your advantage. Especially if you're crying and in a lot of anguish, determine in a flash what's worth keeping, and visualize it like this: you are a burning building. If you could rush into yourself and save only a handful of things to take to a new you, what will they be?

Write them down, and set the list aside until you feel more rational. Then

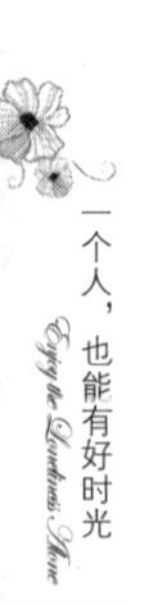

所以，当我觉得不被人关心时，我会迅速浏览一下“赞美集册”，并把所发生的事情记在脑海里：以前有人关心我，他们还会继续关心我。也许最重要的是，通过意识到这一点，我也开始关心我自己。这个过程从未能立马奏效。正如老生常谈但又真实的谚语所说，一个人不会突然间“重新振作起来”，这“需要时间”。不过，事实就是这样。

放弃值得丢弃的东西

负担是孤独的同伴。一些人想拥有更多的社会生活，但这些都被激烈的竞争破坏了，或者因自身产生的恐惧而望而却步。丢弃我通常所说的“废物”（享受生活所不必要的废物），你就会有空闲去做更有意义的事情（保持阅读！）。少些担忧意味着有更多自由，来探索自我和从事自己的兴趣所在。

为什么这听起来是这么显而易见的事？因为事实本就如此。但它可能只在感情波动的某一时期如此，这样你就能集中力量来解放你自己。

不要过度地思考——那会使事情变得更糟。正如许多杰出的演员所知，反复锻炼被谐称为“第二天性”，或者即将在过往经验的基础上有所超越，这和“肌肉记忆”一样富有争议。

当你发现自己特别紧张或忧虑时，除了不愉快的时刻，你可以使用你的一切来改善自己的状况。特别是当你在哭泣和特别痛苦时，找出值得保留的瞬间，像这样来想象：你是一栋正在燃烧的大楼。如果你能冲入自己的内心，并只能拯救少数东西来成就一个崭新的自己，它们会是什么？

把它们写下来，并且把清单放在一旁，直到你感觉更加理性。然后再看一遍，把你现在的思想和当时的感觉集中起来。这会是一个强有力的锻

look at it again, and join your thoughts of the now with what you had felt then. This can be a potent truth-revealing exercise and puts you on the right track.

Find something new worth fighting for

By "fight", I refer not to violence. Rather, I speak of a cause you can champion and stand up for. The "fight" here is versus adversity. Your cause may be a charity that improves others' lives, or even a campaign to save a TV show. Notice how these purposes require others to get involved—they're inherently social, and even though you may not think about so much about that (and shouldn't), they'll lead to you interacting with others, feeling less lonely.

Being recognized as a maverick and a leader isn't a deliberate process you need to set up like a goal. Rather, the goals here are more about the innate satisfaction and happiness you'll feel.

炼，它会让你走上正确的轨道。

找出一些新的值得奋斗的事

“奋斗”，我指的不是暴力。相反，我说的是你能为之奋斗和坚持的目标。这里的“奋斗”是针对逆境而言的。你的目标可能是改善他人生活的宽容，甚至是保存一份电视节目的活动。注意这些目标是怎样要求他人的参与——他们的本质是社会性的，即使你可能没有（也不该）想这么多，但它们会让你和其他人交流配合，让你感觉不那么孤独。

被视为一个标新立异的人和领导者不是一个审慎的过程，你不必设立一个像这样的目标。在一定程度上，这里的目标更多是你所感觉到的满意度和幸福感。

Chapter 4

爱在转角，拥抱幸福

The reasonable man adapts himself to the world; the unreasonable one persists in trying to adapt the world to himself.

明白事理的人使自己适应世界；不明事理的人想使世界适应自己。

丑八怪

© Karen G. Stone

Everyone in the apartment complex I lived in knew who Ugly was. Ugly was the resident tomcat. Ugly loved three things in this world: fighting, eating garbage, and, shall we say, love.

The combination of these things combined with a life spent outside had their effect on Ugly. To start with, he had only one eye and where the other should have been was a gaping hole. He was also missing his ear on the same side, his left foot appeared to have been badly broken at one time, and had healed at an unnatural angle, making him look like he was always turning the corner. His tail has long ago been lost, leaving only the smallest stub, which he would constantly jerk and twitch.

Ugly would have been a dark grey tabby, striped-type, except for the sores covering his head, neck, even his shoulders with thick, yellowing scabs. Every time someone saw Ugly there was the same reaction. "That's one UGLY cat!"

All the children were warned not to touch him, the adults threw rocks at him, hosed him down, squirted him when he tried to come in their home or shut his paws in the door when he would not leave. Ugly always had the same reaction. If you turned the hose on him, he would stand there, getting soaked

名人语库

Only ones among you who will be really happy are those who will have sought and found how to serve.

A. Schweizer

有一点我是知道的：在你们之中，只有那些愿意寻求发现如何为别人服务的人，才是真正幸福的。

施韦策（法国人道主义学者）

我住的公寓大楼里的每个人都认识这只丑八怪。丑八怪曾经是小区里的流浪猫。在这个世上它只爱做三件事：战斗、吃垃圾，还有，应该说是爱。

这三件事再加上在外的流浪生活，造就了这只丑八怪。第一，它只有一只眼睛，另一只则成了一个大窟窿。另外，它也失去了同一侧的耳朵，它的一只左脚似乎也受过伤，痊愈后形成了个极不自然的斜角，使它看起来像是总在不停转弯。它的尾巴也早已不见了，只留下一个短小的砻，像是始终在不停地抽搐着。

丑八怪应该是一条深灰色的虎斑猫，有条纹的品种，只是头上、颈部和肩膀上长着厚厚的黄痂子。每次有人看到丑八怪都是同样的反应："真难看的猫！"

所有的孩子们都被警告不要去碰它，大人们朝它扔石头，用水管浇它；当它准备回屋时用水枪射它，当它不肯离开时用门挤它的爪子。但是，丑八怪永远都是同样的反应。如果你用水管浇它，它就站在那儿被淋得浑身湿透，直到你放弃为止。如果你朝它扔东西，它就会把瘦长的身体蜷缩在

until you gave up and quit. If you threw things at him, he would curl his lanky body around feet in forgiveness.

Whenever he spied children, he would come running, meowing frantically and bump his head against their hand begging for their love. If you ever picked him, up he would immediately begin suckling on your shirt, earring whatever he could find.

One day Ugly shared his love with the neighbor's huskies. They did not respond kindly, and Ugly was badly mauled. From my apartment I could hear his scream and I tried to rush to his aid. By the time I got to where he was laying, it was apparent Ugly's sad life was almost at an end.

Ugly lay in a wet circle, his back legs and lower back twisted grossly out of shape, a gaping tear in the white strip of fur that ran down his front. As I picked him up and tried to carry him home, I could hear him wheezing and gasping, and could feel him struggling. It must be hurting him terribly, I thought.

Then I felt a familiar tugging, sucking sensation on my ear. Ugly, in so much pain, suffering and obviously dying, was trying to suckle my ear. I pulled him closer to me, and he bumped the palm of my hand with his head, then he turned his one golden eye towards me, and I could hear the distinct sound of purring. Even in the greatest pain, that ugly battled-scarred cat was asking only for a little affection, perhaps some compassion.

At that moment I thought Ugly was the most beautiful, loving creature I had ever seen. Never once did he try to bite or scratch me, or even try to get away from me, or struggle in any way. Ugly just looked up at me completely trusting in me to relieve his pain.

Ugly died in my arms before I could get inside, but I sat and held him for a long time afterward thinking about how one scarred, deformed little stray could

脚上，带着它那颗早已宽恕的心。

每当它看到孩子时，都会跑过去，喵呜喵呜地疯狂喊叫，并用它的头使劲蹭孩子们的手，乞求他们的怜爱。如果你把它抱起来，它马上就会开始吸吮你的衬衫、耳环，吸吮任何它能找到的东西。

一天，丑八怪将爱分享给了邻居家的哈士奇们。但对方并没有报以友善，小丑被撕咬得很严重。我在公寓里听见了它的尖叫声，便试图去救它。然而，当我到了它躺着的地方，却看到它悲惨的一生似乎走到了尽头。

丑八怪躺在一个湿漉漉的水坑里，它的后腿和下背严重扭曲在一起，皮毛的白色条纹上有一个大口子也被撕到了前身。当我抱起它，试图带它回家时，还可以听到它的喘息，还可以感到它在挣扎。我知道，它一定伤得太重了。

突然，我感到一阵熟悉的拖拽，我的耳朵上有了被吸吮的感觉。丑八怪，正遭受着这么大的痛苦，甚至已经濒临死亡，竟在努力地舔我的耳朵。我让它靠近我，它便开始用它的头蹭我的手掌，然后，用那只金黄色的眼睛看着我，我可以清楚地听到那几近衰竭的呼吸声。尽管遭受着最剧烈的痛苦，这只丑陋的满身战伤的猫，只是在乞求一点点的爱，或者只是一点点的同情。

在那一刻，我觉得丑八怪是我所见过的最美丽、最可爱的家伙。它从来没试图咬过或抓过我，甚至都没有试着躲避我，或者肆意挣扎。它只是抬头看着我以减轻它的痛苦，对我充满了信任。

在我还没进门时，丑八怪就死在了我的怀里，之后我抱着它坐了很长时间，我在想，一只满身疤痕的畸形小流浪猫，它是如何改变了我对纯净

so alter my opinion about what it means to have true pureness of spirit, to love so totally and truly. Ugly taught me more about giving and compassion than a thousand book, lecture or talk show specials ever could, and for that I will always be thankful. He had been scarred on the outside, but I was scarred on the inside, and it was time for me to move on and learn to love truly and deeply. To give my total to those I cared for.

Many people want to be richer, more successful, well liked, beautiful, but for me, I will always try to be Ugly.

心灵的理解——爱得如此彻底、如此真诚。丑八怪教会我的付出和慈悲胜过读千万本书、听千万次演讲或脱口秀节目，也正因如此，我将永远心存感激。它的伤痕烙在了外表上，而我的内心却早已伤痕累累，是时候忘记过去、往前看，学会爱得真诚、爱得深刻了。我要将我的所有给予那些我在乎的人。

很多人想变得更富有、更成功、更迷人、更美丽；而我，将永远去试着做一只丑八怪。

Always Changing
人生处处是转角

◎ Anonymous

Please excuse me if I'm a little pensive today.

Mark is leaving, and I'm feeling kind of sad.

You probably don't know Mark, but you might be lucky enough to know someone just like him. He's been the heart and soul of the office for a couple of year combining exemplary professional skills with a sweet nature and gentle disposition. He's never been all that interested in getting credit for the terrific work he does. He just wants to do his job, and to do it superbly well.

And now he's moving on to an exciting new professional opportunity. It sounds like it could be the chance of a lifetime, and we're genuinely, sincerely pleased for him. But that doesn't make it any easier to say goodbye to a dear friend and trusted colleague.

Life has a way of throwing these curve balls at us. Just when we start to get comfortable with a person, a place or a situation, something comes along to alter the recipe. A terrific neighbor moves away. Someone in the family graduates. A child finds new love and loyalties through marriage. The family's principle bread-winner is laid off.

Our ability to cope with change and disruption determine to a great degree,

名人语库

Growth and change are the law of all life. Yesterday's answers are inadequate for today's problems—just as the solutions of today will not fill the needs of tomorrow.

Franklin Roosevelt

生长与变化是一切生命的法则。昨日的答案不适用于今日的问题——正如今天的方法不能解决明天的需求。

罗斯福 .F.（美国总统）

如果我今天有点忧郁，请原谅我。

马克要走了，我感到有些难过。

你可能不认识马克，但如果你认识像他那样的人，你可就走运了。好几年来，他都是办公室里的核心和灵魂人物，专业技能堪称模范，态度和蔼，性格温和。他的工作表现十分出色，却对于争风邀功从无兴趣。他只想做他的工作，并能出色地完成。

而现在，他要向一份令人振奋的新职迈进。这听起来就像 个千载难逢的机会，我们也真心诚挚地替他高兴。但是，那并没使我们跟这样一位亲爱的朋友、信任的同事告别来得容易些。

生活用它的方式不断向我们抛出曲线球。当我们刚开始与某人融洽相处，或是适应一个地方或一种情境时，某事就发生了，并改变了这种境况。很棒的邻居要搬家了。某个家庭成员要毕业了。孩子们找到新欢，通过婚姻找到忠诚。家庭的支柱失业了。

我们应付变化和混乱的能力，在很大程度上决定了我们生活的安宁、

our peace, happiness and contentment in life.

But how do we do that? Philosophers have considered the question for centuries and their responses have been varied. According to the author of the Biblical book of Ecclesiaste, comfort can be found in remembering that "to every thing there is a season, and a time to every purpose under heaven." Kahlil Gibran urged his listeners to "let today embrace the past with remembrance, and the future with longing".

A friend of mine who works for the government is fond of reminding his fellow bureaucrats that "survivabi-lity depends upon adaptability". And then there's Chris, the California surf-rat, who once told me that the answer to life's problems can be summed up in four words: "Go with the flow."

"It's like surfing," Chris explained. "You can't organize the ocean. Waves just happen. You ride 'em where they take you, then you paddle back out there and catch the next one. Sure, you're always hoping for the perfect wave where you can get, like, you know, totally tubular. But mostly you just take 'em the way they come. It's not like you're trying to nail Jell-O to a tree, you know?"

I'm not exactly sure, but I think Chris was saying that life is a series of events—both good and bad. No matter how deft your organizational skill there will always be life-influencing factors over which you have no control. The truly successful person expects the unexpected, and is prepared to make adjustments should the need arise—as it almost always does.

That doesn't mean you don't keep trying to make all your dreams come true. It just means that when things come up that aren't exactly in your plan, you work around them—and then you move on. Of course, some bumps along the road of life are easier to take than others. A rained-out picnic, for example, is easier to cope with than the sudden death of a loved one. But the principle is

幸福和满意度。

但我们应该怎么做？哲学家们已经思考这个问题好几个世纪了，而他们的回答各有不同。根据《圣经·旧约全书·传道书》的作者，人们可以通过记住“大千世界，万物皆有时”来获得安慰。而卡里·纪伯伦也曾敦促他的听众去“让今日用记忆拥抱过去，用渴望拥抱未来”。

我一个在政府工作的朋友喜欢提醒他那帮官僚同事们“生存取决于适应性”。还有克里斯，加利福尼亚州的一位冲浪爱好者，他曾告诉我说，生活中所有问题的答案都可以总结为四个字——“顺其自然”。

“就像冲浪，”克里斯解释道，“你无法掌控大海。波浪随时都可能荡起。你乘浪而行，任随它领你前行，然后，你伏身于冲浪板往回，接而踏乘下一个浪。当然，你总会希望等到那个完美的浪头，就像你知道的那种滚筒浪。但大多数情况，也就是随波逐流，这并不是什么登天难事，知道吗？”

我不太确定，但我想克里斯是在说，生活是由一连串事件组成的——其中有好也有坏。无论你的组织技能有多娴熟，总会有些你无法控制的因素在影响你的生活。真正的成功者能够预计意料之外的事，并准备好在必要时作出调整——这种情况总是发生。

那并不意味着你不需要不断努力使你的梦想成真。它只是说，当计划之外的事发生时，你得去应付，然后继续前行。当然，人生沿途出现的一些波折要比另一些容易处理。比如，因为下雨要取消野餐，总比自己所爱的人突然去世更容易应付。但原则是相同的。

“的确，改变会给人带来痛苦，但改变却是永远必须的。”哲学家托马斯·卡莱尔说道，“而且，如果记忆拥有力量和价值，那么希望也同样

the same.

"Change, indeed, is painful, yet ever needful," said philosopher Thomas Carlyle. "And if memory have its force and worth, so also has hope."

We're going to miss Mark, just like you'll miss that graduate, that neighbor or that newlywed. But rather than dwell on the sadness of our parting, we'll focus on our hopes for a brighter future—for him, and for us. And then we'll go out and do everything we can to make that future happen.

Until our plans change—again.

拥有。”

我们会想念马克，就像你会想念毕业离家的孩子、那位搬走的邻居或那新婚的儿女一样。但我们与其沉湎于离别带来的悲伤，不如把期望专注于一个更光明的未来——为他，也为我们自己。然后，我们将走出去，尽我们所能，去实现梦想中的未来。

直到我们的计划——再次改变。

At the Edge of the Sea
海边漫步

◎ Rachel Carson

The shore is an ancient world, for as long as there has been an earth and sea there has been this place of the meeting of land and water. Yet it is a world that keeps alive the sense of continuing creation and of the relentless drive of life. Each time that I enter it, I gain some new awareness of its beauty and its deeper meanings, sensing that intricate fabric of life by which one creature is linked with another, and each with its surroundings.

In my thoughts of the shore, one place stands apart for its revelation of exquisite beauty. It is a pool hidden within a cave that one can visit only rarely and briefly when the lowest of the year's low tides fall below it, and perhaps from that very fact it acquires some of its special beauty. Choosing such a tide , I hoped for a glimpse of the pool.

The ebb was to fall early in the morning. I knew that if the wind held from the northwest and no interfering swell ran in from a distant storm the level of the sea should drop below the entrance to the pool. There had been sudden ominous showers in the night, with rain like handfuls of gravel flung on the roof. When I looked out into the early morning the sky was full of a gray dawn light but the sun had not yet risen. Water and air were pallid. Across the bay the moon was a luminous disc in the western sky, suspended above the dim line of distant shore—

名人语库

Time is a versatile performer. It flies, marches on, heals all wounds, runs out and will tell.

Franklin P. Jones

时间是个多才多艺的表演者。它能展翅飞翔，能阔步前进，能治愈创伤，能消逝而去，也能揭示真相。

富兰克林·P. 琼斯（美国作家）

海岸是一个古老的世界，自从有地球和海洋以来，就有这个水陆相接的地方。然而，人们却感觉它是一个总在创造、生机勃勃而又精力充沛的世界。每一次，当我踏入这个世界，感觉到生物之间以及每一个生物与它的环境之间，通过错综复杂的生命结构彼此相连的时候，我对它的美，对它的深层涵义，都会产生一些新的认识。

每当我想起海岸，就有一个地方因它所展现出的独特美妙而显得出类拔萃。那就是一个隐匿于洞穴中的水潭。平时，这个洞被海水所淹没，一年之中只有潮汐降落至最低、低于水潭时，人们才能在这罕有的短暂时刻看见它。也许正因如此，它获得了某种特殊的美。我选好这样一个低潮的时机，希望能看一眼水潭。

潮水将在清晨时分退下去。我知道，如果不刮西北风，远处的风暴不再掀起惊涛骇浪进行干扰，海平面就会低于水潭的入口。夜间突然下了几场不祥的阵雨，一把把碎石般的雨点被抛到屋顶上。清晨，我望着天空笼罩着灰蒙蒙的曙光，太阳还没有升起。水和空气一片暗淡。一轮明月挂在海湾对面西边的天空上，月下昏暗的一线就是远方的海岸——8 月的望月把海潮吸得很低，直到那与世隔离的海洋世界的门槛。当我观望的时候，一只海鸥飞过云杉之上。呼之欲出的太阳把它的腹部照映成粉色。终于，

the full August moon, drawing the tide to the low, low levels of the threshold of the alien sea world. As I watched, a gull flew by, above the spruces. Its breast was rosy with the light of the unrisen sun. The day was, after all, to be fair.

Later, as I stood above the tide near the entrance to the pool, the promise of that rosy light was sustained. From the base of the steep wall of rock on which I stood, a moss covered ledge jutted seaward into deep water. In the surge at the rim of the ledge the dark fronds of oarweeds swayed smooth and gleaming as leather. The projecting ledge was the path to the small hidden cave and its pool. Occasionally a swell, stronger than the rest, rolled smoothly over the rim and broke in foam against the cliff. But the intervals between such swells were long enough to admit me to the ledge and long enough for a glimpse of that fairy pool, so seldom and so briefly exposed.

And so I knelt on the wet carpet of sea moss and looked back into the dark cavern that held the pool in a shallow basin. The floor of the cave was only a few inches below the roof, and a mirror had been created in which all that grew on the ceiling was reflected in the still water below.

Under water that was clear as glass the pool was carpeted with green sponge. Gray patches of sea squirts glistened on the ceiling and colonies of raft coral were a pale apricot color. In the moment when I looked into the cave a little elfin starfish hung down, suspended by the merest thread, perhaps by only a single tube foot. It reached down to touch its own reflection, so perfectly delineated that there might have been, not one starfish, but two. The beauty of the reflected images and of the limpid pool itself was the poignant beauty of things that are ephemeral, existing only until the sea should rcturn to fill the little cave.

天晴了。

后来，当我站在高于海潮的水潭入口处时，四周已是瑰红色的晨光。从我立脚的峭岩底部，一块被青苔覆盖的礁石伸向大海深处。海水拍击着礁石周围，水藻上下左右地漂动，像皮革般光滑发亮。通往隐藏的小洞和洞中水潭的路径是那些凸现的暗礁。间或一阵强于一阵的波涛悠然地漫过礁石的边缘，并在岩壁上击成水沫。这种波涛间歇的时间足以让我踏上礁石，足以让我瞥见那仙境般的水潭，那平时很少露面、露面也只是一瞬的水潭。

我跪在那海苔铺成的潮湿地毯上，向那些黑洞里窥探，就是这些黑洞把水潭环抱成一个浅盆模样。洞底距离顶部只有几英寸，真是一面天造明镜。洞顶上的一切生物都倒映在底下平静的水中。

清明如镜的水底铺满了一层碧绿的海绵。一片片灰色的海蛸在洞顶上闪闪发光，一堆堆软珊瑚披着淡淡的杏黄色衣裳。就在我朝洞里探望的那一刻，从洞顶上挂下一只小海星，仅仅悬在一条线上，或许就在它的一只管足上。它向下触碰着自己的倒影。多么完美的画面！仿佛不是一只海星，而是一对海星。美丽的倒影，清澈的水潭，这些转眼即逝的事物所体现的强烈而动人的美——一旦海水漫过小洞，这种美便不复存在了。

Leaving Work to Gaze at Sunsets
夕阳无限好

◎ Laurie Granieri

I believe in leaving work at five o'clock.

In a nation that operates on a staunch Protestant work ethic, this belief could be considered radical. Working only 40 hours a week? I just don't know many people who punch out at five o'clock anymore. It seems downright quaint, like pocket watches and shoe shines.

My father tried to teach me the importance of hard work, long hours and dedication to a career. But then there are the things he taught me unintentionally, like when he arrived home from work for the last time and crawled up the stairs.

My father, a self-employed sales trainer, was that sick, that tired. His body was wracked with liver cancer, and he suffered the effects of a diabetic ulcer. Still, he insisted on traveling to honor his commitment to give a seminar. He probably earned a lot of money that day, and he paid the price: He returned to the hospital soon after and was dead within three months, at age 58.

It's been 10 years since I saw my father come home that night and since then, I've thought a lot about work. I've decided something: I will never crawl up the stairs. As much as I love my job as a newspaper reporter, I will never work myself into the ground, literally or figuratively.

名人语库

Ordinary people merely think how they shall spend their time; a man of talent tries to use it.

Arthur Schopenhauer

普通人只想到如何度过时间，有才能的人设法利用时间。

叔本华（德国哲学家）

我的信念是在 5 点钟结束每天的工作。

在这个奉行新教徒那套“工作至上”理念的国度，我的这一信念可被视为激进主义了。每周只工作 40 小时？我认识的人中很少是下午 5 点打卡下班的。那看起来十足的怪异，就跟怀表、鞋油这类古老的东西一样。

我父亲尽力教导我努力工作、超时工作以及献身事业这几点的重要性。但后来，他也无意中教了我一些东西，比如那次——他最后一次下班回家爬上楼梯的时候。

我父亲是一名自由的销售培训师。那时，他病得很厉害，十分疲惫。肝癌拖垮了他的身体，他还饱受糖尿病溃疡的折磨。不过，他为履行承诺仍坚持到外地主持一个研讨会。他那天可能赚了不少钱，但他也付出了代价：不久之后又住进了医院，而且三个月后就去世了，年仅 58 岁。

从那晚看到父亲回家直到现在，已经过去 10 年了，自那以后，我对工作作了多番思考。我决定了一件事：我决不爬楼梯回家。作为一名报社记者，尽管我非常热爱我的工作，但我永远不会因为拼命工作而把自己送进“坟墓”里，无论是字面上还是比喻的意义。

The idea of leaving work at work didn't come easily to me. After all, I am my father's daughter. In college, I wasn't going to keg parties in a frat basement; I was the girl who lingered on the library steps each morning, waiting for the doors to open. I even dreamt about schoolwork.

My dad once told me he was unable to just gaze at a sunset; he had to be doing something as he looked at it—writing, reading, playing chess. You could say he was a success: He was a published author, an accomplished musician, fluent in German and the American Sign Language. That's an impressive list, but here's the thing: I want to gaze at sunsets. I don't want to meet a deadline during them or be writing a column at the same time, or glance at them over the top of a book.

This raises the question: If I leave work at five o' clock to watch the sunset, what are the consequences? Do I risk not reaching the top of my profession? Maybe, because honestly, knocking off after eight hours probably won't earn me the corner office or the lucrative promotion.

But hey, leaving work at five o' clock means I eat dinner with my family. I get to hop on my bike and pedal through the streets of my hometown as the shadows lengthen and the traffic thins. And I get to take in a lot of sunsets. That's got to be worth something.

只在工作时间内工作的想法于我并非易事。毕竟，有其父必有其女。读大学时，我不参加在地下室里举办的大学生联谊会，而是每天早上就逗留在图书馆的阶梯上，等着图书馆开门。我甚至做梦都会梦见写作业。

我的父亲曾经告诉我，他没法只是凝视着夕阳；看着夕阳的同时他还得做些别的事——写作、阅读、下棋。你可以称他为成功人士：他是一名出版过作品的作家，一位有成就的音乐家，能说流利的德语，能熟练运用美国手语。这一连串成就看起来让人印象深刻，但问题来了：我想凝视夕阳。我不想边看夕阳边赶在最后期限前完成工作，也不想边看夕阳边给专栏赶稿，又或者是看着书，偶尔才朝那抹夕阳瞥上一眼。

这就引发了一个问题：如果我 5 点就下班去看夕阳，会有什么后果？我是否就无法爬到职场最高位？也许是，因为老实说，工作 8 小时就下班，想搬进角落里的高层办公室或升职加薪是不太可能的。

不过，嘿，5 点就下班意味着我能和家人共进晚餐。我跳上单车，穿梭在家乡的街道上，一切都被拉长了影子，路上车少人稀。从此，我看了不少夕阳美景。我觉得这样做是值得的。

4 Goals for Perfect Life

完美人生四大梦

◎ Brian Tracy

Healthy and Fit

The first goal common to all of us is health and energy. We all want to be healthy and fit, to have high levels of energy and to live free of pain and illness. Today, with the incredible advances in medical science, the quality of our health and fitness, and our lifespan, is largely determined by design, not by chance. People with excellent health habits are far healthier, have more energy, and live longer and better than people who have poor health habits.

Excellent Relationships

The second goal that we all have in common is to enjoy excellent relationships—intimate, personal or social—with the people we like and respect, and who like, love and respect us in turn. Fully 85% of your happiness will be determined by the quality of your relationships at each stage, and in each area, of your life. How well you get along with people, and how much they like, love and respect you, has more impact on the quality of your life than perhaps any other factor.

名人语库

A man can succeed at almost anything for which he has unlimited enthusiasm.

C. M. Schwab

只要有无限的热情，一个人几乎可以在任何事情上取得成功。

施瓦布（美国实业家）

健康有活力

我们的人生第一大梦就是身体健康、精力充沛。我们都希望自己健康，活力无穷，远离痛苦和疾病。今天，医学的进步令人难以置信，我们的身体质量、健康状况、寿命长短，很大程度上取决于良好的规划，而非偶然性。有优良生活习惯的人，比那些糟蹋自己身体的人，能活得更健康、精力更旺盛、寿命更长久。

优秀的人际关系

我们的人生第二大梦，就是完美的人际关系——与亲人、密友、社会上的其他人融洽相处——我们喜爱且尊敬的人，也是喜爱且尊敬我们的人。人们在任何一个人生阶段，或居住在任何一个地区是否觉得幸福快乐，其中 85% 取决于人际关系的好坏。你与他人相处的情形，他人是否喜欢你、爱你、尊重你，这比其他因素更加影响你的生活质量。

Do What You Love

The third common goal is to do work that we enjoy, to do it well, and to be well paid for it. You want to be able to get and keep the job you want, to get paid more and promoted faster. You want to earn the very most that is possible for you at each stage of your career, whatever you do.

Achieve Financial Independence

The fourth goal we all have in common is to achieve financial independence. You want to reach the point in life where you have enough money so that you never have to worry about money again. You want to be completely free of financial worries. You want to be able to order dinner in a restaurant without using the price listings to determine what you want to eat.

If you can dream it, you can achieve it!

从事自己喜欢的工作

人生第三大梦，就是做自己喜欢的工作，而且工作出色，薪酬优厚。你希望能够从事自己喜欢的行业，拥有喜欢的工作，可以得到晋升、领取更多的报酬。不论你从事哪一个行业，你都希望在职场生涯的每一个阶段尽可能赚取更多。

财务独立

人生的第四个大梦就是达到财务独立。你想要赚取相当数量的财富，这样你一辈子都无须再为钱担忧。你想要完全摆脱财务上的烦恼。走进任何一家餐厅，你希望可以随心所欲点餐享用，而不用留意价目表上的数字。

只要你敢于梦想，就能实现！

Butterfly Effect
人生中的蝴蝶效应

◎ Erin E.

"Thank you for your application. We would like to congratulate you," the letter read. Those words can make your heart skip a beat and bring tears to your eyes. The feeling of following your dreams is inexplicable and proof that all your hard work was worth it.

It is a signpost in life, a trail marker. It is a day you will never forget, the day you opened that envelope and your future was revealed. But what about all those days in-between—the ones that make and break you, the days that are nothing special.

Would you have received that acceptance letter had you not attended the college fair at your school? What if you had forgotten to send an essay with your application, would you have been rejected?

In life, one step creates the next. Each day is of equal importance, no matter how good or bad. There is no moment in life that does not matter. Regardless of how insignificant, each choice, each day, each idea, is the birth of the next. Something simple can completely reshape your life. It's just like the Butterfly Effect and you never know what is at the end. To go back in time and change one moment in the many that create your life could change everything that follows.

名人语库

It never will rain roses. When we want to have more roses we must plant trees.

G. Eliot

天上永远不会掉下玫瑰来，如果想要更多的玫瑰，必须自己种植。

艾略特（英国小说家）

“感谢你的申请。我们要恭喜你。”信上写道。那些话能使你的心为之一颤，让你热泪盈眶。追随梦想的感觉是难以言喻的，而且证明你所有的努力都是值得的。

这是人生路上的一个标记，一个里程碑。这一天你永远都不会忘记，你打开那个信封，你的未来随之展现。但是，在你获得录取信之前的所有日子呢——那些使你成功也使你崩溃的日子，那些平凡的日子。

如果那时你没有参加学校的学院展，你还会收到录取信吗？如果当时在申请书上忘记附上一篇个人陈述，你会被拒绝吗？

人生中，步步相随。无论好与坏，每一天都一样重要。人生中没有一个时刻是无关紧要的。不管如何不值一提，每个选择、每一天、每个想法，都会引出下一步。简单的事情可以完全重塑你的人生。就像是蝴蝶效应，你永远不知道最后的结果是什么。若回顾从前，改变创造你人生众多时刻中的一个，随后的一切也会被改变。

If I've learned anything, it is that everything matters. You can struggle through life in an attempt to create the perfect path, but the truth is you will always wonder if it could have been better. Everything is important and nothing need be changed—to climb up the hill may be difficult, but you'll reach the top no matter which path you choose.

要是说我悟出什么道理，那就是任何事情都是重要的。你可以奋斗一生，试图创造完美的人生之路，但事实是，你总是怀疑可能还有更好的路可走。每件事情都是重要的，任何事情都无需改变——爬山的过程可能很艰辛，但无论你选择哪条道路，你终会到达顶峰。

Choosing Life

选择你的生活

◎ Anonymous

Michael is the kind of guy you love to hate. He is always in a good mood and always has something positive to say. When someone would ask him how he was doing, he would reply, "If I were any better, I would be twins!" He was a natural motivator.

If an employee was having a bad day, Michael was there telling the employee how to look on the positive side of the situation. Seeing his style really made me curious, so one day I went up to Michael and asked him, "I don't get it. You can't be a positive person all of the time. How do you do it?"

Michael replied, "Each morning I wake up and say to myself, 'You have two choices today. You can choose to be in a good mood or you can choose to be in a bad mood.' I choose to be in a good mood. Each time something bad happens, I can choose to be a victim or I can choose to learn from it. I choose to learn from it. Every time someone comes to me complaining, I can choose to accept their complaining or I can point out the positive side of life. I choose the positive side of life."

"Yeah, right, it's not that easy," I protested.

"Yes, it is," Michael said. "Life is all about choices. When you cut away all

名人语库

Joys are our wings, sorrows are our spurs.

Jean Paul Richter

欢乐是我们的双翼，悲痛是我们的动力。

里克特 · J.P.（法国作家）

迈克尔是那种让你又爱又恨的家伙。他总是喜笑颜开的，总是说些积极上进的话。如果有人问他近况如何，他会回答说："如果我还能再好的话，我就成双胞胎了！"他是个天生的乐天派。

如果哪位雇员某天过得很不顺，迈克尔就会告诉他如何看待事情的光明面。他的这种方式着实让我好奇，所以有一天，我找到迈克尔，问他："我真弄不明白。你怎么能时时刻刻都那样积极乐观？你是如何做到的？"

迈克尔回答说："每天早晨醒来时，我对自己说，'今天你有两种选择。你可以选择心情愉快，你也可以选择心情恶劣。'我选择心情愉快。每次发生什么糟糕的事情时，我可以选择成为一个受害者，也可以选择从中吸取教训。我选择从中吸取教训。每当有人向我抱怨什么时，我可以选择接受他们的抱怨，也可以选择指出生活的积极面。我选择指出生活的积极面。"

"是啊，不错，可它并不那么容易呀。"我表示异议。

"其实很容易，"迈克尔说，"生活就是选择。拨开纷繁的表象来看，生

the junk, every situation is a choice. You choose how you react to situations. You choose how people affect your mood. You choose to be in a good mood or bad mood. The bottom line: It's your choice how you live your life."

I reflected on what Michael said. Soon after, I left the Tower Industry to start my own business. We lost touch, but I often thought about him when I decided to choose life instead of reacting to it.

Several years later, I heard that Michael was involved in a serious accident, falling some 60 feet from a communications tower. After 18 hours of surgery and weeks of intensive care, Michael was released from the hospital with rods placed in his back. I saw Michael about six months after the accident. When I asked him how he was, he replied. "If I were any better, I'd be twins. Wanna see my scars?"

I declined to see his wounds, but I did ask him what had gone through his mind as the accident took place. "The first thing that went through my mind was the well-being of my soon to be born daughter," Michael replied. "Then, as I lay on the ground, I remembered that I had two choices: I could choose to live or I could choose to die. I chose to live."

"Weren't you scared? Did you lose consciousness?" I asked.

Michael continued, "The paramedics were great. They kept telling me I was going to be fine. But when they wheeled me into the ER and I saw the expressions on the faces of the doctors and nurses, I got really scared. In their eyes, I read 'He's a dead man.' I knew I needed to take action."

"What did you do?" I asked.

"Well, there was a big burly nurse shouting questions at me," said Michael. "She asked if I was allergic to anything. 'Yes,' I replied. The doctors and nurses stopped working as they waited for my reply. I took a deep breath and yelled, 'Gravity.' Over their laughter, I told them, 'I am choosing to live. Operate on me

活的每种境遇都是一种选择。你选择如何应付生活中的种种情形。你选择人们怎样影响你的情绪。你选择是心情愉快还是心情恶劣。说到底：如何生活是你自己的选择。”

我琢磨着迈克尔的这席话。不久之后，我离开了大企业的工作岗位，去开创自己的事业。我们失去了联系，但当我决定主动选择生活而非被动应对生活时，我时常想起迈克尔。

几年之后，我听说迈克尔遭遇一场恶性事故，从一座通讯大楼的 60 英尺高处掉了下来。在经历了 18 个小时的手术和数周的精心护理之后，迈克尔出院了，他的背部装上了金属杆。大约事故半年之后，我见到了迈克尔。当我问他怎么样时，他回答说，“如果我还能再好，我就成双胞胎了。想看看我的伤疤吗？”

我拒绝看他的伤痕，但是问了他当事故发生时他是怎么想的。“我首先想到的，就是我那即将出世的女儿——她的幸福，”迈克尔答道，“然后，当我躺在地上时，我记得当时我有两种选择：我可以选择活着，也可以选择死。我选择了活着。”

“你难道不害怕吗？你当时失去知觉了吗？”我问。

迈克尔继续说道：“那些护理人员棒极了。他们不停地告诉我，我会没事的。但当他们把我推进急救室时，我看到医生和护士脸上的表情，还真是吓坏了。在他们的眼里，我读出了‘他是个死人。’我知道我应该有所行动了。”

“你做了什么？”我问道。

“有一位人高马大的护士大声冲我问问题，”迈克尔说，“她问我是否对什么过敏。‘是的。’我回答说。医生和护士都停下手中的工作，等着我回

as if I am alive, not dead. '"

Michael lived, thanks to the skill of his doctors, but also because of his amazing attitude. I learned from him that every day we have the choice to live fully.

答。我深吸一口气，大声说，‘万有引力！’他们的笑声未了，我便告诉他们，‘我要活下去。把我当成个活人而不是死人来做手术。’”

迈克尔活了下来，这要感谢那些医生的高明医术，但也要归功于他那令人赞叹的态度。我从他那里学会了：我们每天都可以选择充实地活着。

10 Ways to Cheer Up

郁闷时让自己振作的 10 种方法

◎ Anonymous

Feeling a little blue? Ten Ways to Cheer Up. Here are ten fast and easy ways to smile.

1. Play outside

Leave your apartment and go outside. Sun and fresh air are good for you.

2. Exercise

When you exercise, your brain releases a chemical called endorphins. This chemical makes you feel happier. That is just another reason why exercise is good for you.

3. Have a Heart-to-Heart

If something is bothering you, it is a good idea to talk about it. Call a friend or relative. A good chat is great way to feel better fast.

4. Play Pop Music

Westlife, Backstreet Boys, S.H.E…who doesn't like a little mindless pop? Listening to upbeat, happy music will make you smile. Singing along won't hurt either.

5. Laughter is the best medicine

Laughing is the best way to improve your mood. Children laugh around 400

名人语库

Growing old is not upsetting; being perceived as old is.

Kenny Rogers

越来越老并不可怕，可怕的是让人觉得越来越老。

肯尼·罗杰斯（美国乡村歌王）

感觉有些郁闷吗？以下十种方法可以让你振作起来。快速又简单，让你顷刻露出微笑。

1. 外出游玩

离开你的房间，去外面走走吧。享受阳光和新鲜空气，这对你大有好处。

2. 运动

运动时，你的大脑会释放一种叫做内啡肽的化学元素。这种物质会让你感觉更愉悦。这仅仅只是运动对你有好处的原因之一。

3. 促膝谈心

如果你正因什么事而烦恼，有个好建议就是大声把它说出来。给你的某个亲朋好友打电话。一次好的谈心可以让你迅速好起来。

4. 演奏流行音乐

西城男孩，后街男孩，S.H.E……谁不喜欢点儿轻松的流行乐呢？听听那些欢快的音乐吧，这些欢快之音能让你快乐起来。跟着歌儿哼唱可不会有任何伤害。

5. 开怀大笑是一剂良药

大笑是改善心情最好的办法。孩子一天大约要笑 400 次。成人一天却

times a day. Adults only laugh about 20 times a day. What happened? Be a kid for a day: play games, watch funny movies, or read jokes online.

6. Power of Chocolate

Chocolate has special natural chemicals that make you happy. Plus, it tastes so good!

7. Draw

Be an artist! Draw, paint, or make something. Even if it is not perfect, being creative relieves stress.

8. Get a dog

Dogs are cute, energetic, and fun. Plus, studies show that people with pets live longer and people with dogs live the longest!

9. Breathe

If you can't go to the gym, try taking deep breaths. Breathing deeply will relax your muscles and give you energy.

10. Think positive

Close your eyes and think of a beautiful scene or a time when you were happy and feeling good.

只笑 20 次。为什么会这样？做一天的孩子吧：玩玩游戏，看看喜剧，或者上网读读笑话。

6. 巧克力的力量

巧克力含有一种可以让人快乐的天然化学物质。另外，它也很美味！

7. 画画

做一回艺术家！画画，涂鸦，或者做点手工。就算做得不那么完美，但创作可以缓解压力。

8. 养一条小狗

狗狗既可爱，又充满活力，而且有趣至极！此外，研究显示养宠物的人活得更长，养狗的人是活得最长的！

9. 呼吸

如果你不能去健身房，那就试试深呼吸。深呼吸可以放松你的肌肉，为你提供能量。

10. 乐观地思考

闭上眼睛，想想那些美丽的画面，或者你感觉最棒的开心时刻。

How to Fall in Love With Yourself
和自己谈场恋爱

◎ Sherri

How to fall in love with yourself? Here are a few ideas you can try to build yourself up and fall in love with yourself all over again.

1. Focus on your strengths. We all have strengths and luckily they are not all the same. Do things you are naturally good at and enjoy and you will build self confidence, efficiency and pride.

2. Be proud of your accomplishments. No matter how big or seemingly small your accomplishments are you should be very proud of each and every one of them. Whether it's completing high school, university, starting your own company, having kids and raising a family, completing a project that's hanging around for far too long, be proud. Celebrate the small and large accomplishments and everything in between.

3. Get excited about who you are. Celebrate your uniqueness. Maybe you're a very caring individual, efficient, or adept to solving problems. Embrace it. Be proud that you're not like everyone else in your social circle. People love you for being you.

4. Share your talent. If you've got a talent share it with the world. If you can write—write, if you can dance—dance, if you can organize…well you get

名人语库

Behavior is a mirror in which every one shows his image.

Johann Wolfgang von Goethe

行为是一面镜子，每个人都把自己的形象显现于其中。

歌德（德国诗人）

如何爱上你自己？这里有一些小贴士，你可以试着振作起来，重新爱上你自己。

1. 专注于自己的强项。我们都有强项，幸运的是，每个人的强项各有千秋。做那些你天生擅长的事情，享受这个过程，你将建立起自信心、高效率和骄傲感。

2. 为自己的成功感到骄傲。不管是大的还是小的成就，你都应该为每一次成就而感到自豪。无论是完成高中学业，大学顺利毕业，还是开了自己的公司，有了孩子，开始抚养家庭，或者是完成了一个拖延已久的项目，这些都值得自豪。庆祝这些大大小小的成就吧。

3. 为你就是你自己而高兴。庆祝你的独一无二。也许你富有爱心，也许你做事高效，又或者你解决问题很老道。拥抱你的独特吧。为此而感到自豪，因为你与你的社交圈里的其他人不同。正因为你就是你，所以大家才会爱你。

4. 分享你的才华。如果你有独特的禀赋，与世界分享它吧。如果你文笔很好——写作吧；如果你舞姿轻盈——跳舞吧；如果你组织能力很强……

the picture. Believe it or not there are people out there who could benefit greatly from you sharing your talents. Ever notice how giving to others makes you feel so incredible about yourself?

5. Forgive yourself. Guilt is a weird thing. All guilt does is hold us in the past reliving something we wish we could change. Not going to happen I'm afraid. Forgiveness is a choice. Forgive yourself. The past is the past (I know you've heard this before but the more you hear it the more you may start to believe it). Forgive yourself, apologize and move on.

6. Do something just for you. Take time for yourself and just relax. Rest both your mind and your body. Rejuvenate by sitting quietly listen to soft soothing music or watch the wonders of nature from your own backyard, balcony or window. Treat yourself to a massage or spa day. Whatever it is that makes you feel special and relaxed...do it.

Love yourself. Take pride in all your unique glory. Maybe you're quirky and have a very different talent. Embrace it. Flaunt it and share it with the world!

嗯，你懂的。不管你相信与否，还有人会因为分享你的才能而大大获益。你有没有注意到，与别人分享的这个过程，会让你感觉如此的奇妙和难以置信?

5. 原谅你自己。内疚是件很奇怪的事情。内疚感只会让我们纠缠于过去不放手，总想着重来一遍，希望可以改变一切。不过这恐怕不会发生。宽恕是一种选择。原谅你自己。过去的已经过去（我知道这句话已经是老生常谈了，但你听到的次数越多，你会越应该相信它）。原谅自己，道歉，然后继续向前。

6. 为自己做些事情。给自己留点时间，只是为了放松一下。让你的身心都好好休息。静静地坐着，听着舒缓的音乐，或从后院、阳台或窗口，欣赏大自然的奇迹。做做按摩或泡泡温泉。不管是什么让你觉得很特别、很放松的事……去做就好。

爱自己，为自己所有独一无二的魅力感到骄傲。也许你有点奇特，有些不同常人的才华，那么，拥抱你的特别吧。要炫耀，然后跟全世界分享。

I desire to be radiant—to radiate life.

我渴望的是发光——让生命放射光芒。